John Christopher

MOLASSES BREAD & TEA

Note for Librarians: A cataloguing record for this book is available from Library and Archives
Canada at www.collectionscanada.ca/amicus/index-e.html
ISBN 1-4120-9575-1

Printed in Victoria, BC, Canada. Printed on paper with minimum 30% recycled fibre.
Trafford's print shop runs on "green energy" from solar, wind and other environmentally-friendly power sources.

Offices in Canada, USA, Ireland and UK

10 9 8 7 6 5 4 3 2 1

Chapter Outline

Victoria St. St.John's, circa 1970 : the author's childhood and boyhood street from the late 1930s
to the late 1950s

SS Caribou in St John's harbour 1938

Biographical note

Newfoundland writer John P Christopher, singer, songwriter, marine biologist sits down to *Molasses Bread and Tea*, his anecdotal account of growing up in St. John's, and experiences of life in Newfoundland out-ports in the 1930's and 1940's. The rugged beauty, hardships and war peril of this era are movingly conveyed. The author's travels then take us to the Canadian North and he details interesting encounters with beluga whales, seals and other wildlife, on the tundra, in the company of Inuit friends. He also documents a gruesome season spent on a seal hunt on board a Norwegian-Canadian sealer where he's called upon to act as ship's doctor in addition to his observational and collecting work for the *Canadian Fisheries Research Board*. Some of his memories are evoked in a selection of photos and these, along with his own lyrics, honour the spirit of the time.

4

The author wishes to thank the Karlsen Shipping Company of Halifax, NS, Canada, Dr. David Sergeant formerly of FRB (Arctic Unit), for giving me the opportunity, residents of Whale Cove, Hudson Bay (1962-63), Marty Corbin and Ken Mackenzie for reading and commenting on the manuscript, and Mary Boyce for considerable help in editing this edition. Thanks also to Jeffery Huan and, Allen Baxter (Central Eglinton Community Centre, Toronto, Ontario)) as well as Normand Houle for their much appreciated computer assistance. Finally, thanks to Farley Mowat for allowing me to cite themes from 'People of the Deer' (Published in 1952), to Beverly Borens for giving me contemporary information about Whale Cove and Frances Ferdinands for allowing me to use her painting 'Quarry', on the book cover.

Molasses Bread and Tea

Conception Bay

Last night I was a 'dreamin',
Of a scene so long ago,
And still it lingers there today,
For it seems it will not go,
Oh! my friend it seemed so near,
It seemed like yesterday,
When father sailed the ocean,
Fished in Conception Bay.

We learned about the fishing,
And when they came to stay,
The caplin brought the herring home,
And they filled their nets that way,
Great their fires on the beach,
Where they worked till the break of day,
For us 'twas just a party time,
Livin' in Conception Bay.

Twas early in the morning,
From work those boys would break,
With bread and 'lassey and cups of tea,
A mug-up time to take,
Songs to warm them while they wait,
For the breakin' of the day,
When horses came to haul the catch,
Up from Conception Bay.

The boys now they've all gone away,
It's not the same today,
I stand upon our hill so high,
I gaze around our bay
Not a man's a'rowin' there,
And there's not the smell of hay,
So I'm livin' in Toronto now, not in Conception Bay.

Part One: Beginnings

When We Were Young

I was first taken out on the waters of St. John's harbour and beyond, by my father. It was an exciting ride for me then, just a 5-year-old boy. This was made in a 20-foot open fishing boat, powered by a single-stroke Grey marine engine that made a funny put-put sound as we went along. After first enjoying the sights and smells of the harbour, we passed through the tiny slit of opening that forms the narrows leading to Freshwater Bay and the open Atlantic. Here the gentle moderate swells of the open sea rolled the small boat and the seas beat a pleasant drum against the bow as we made a wide circle around the Bay. Overhead, several species of seabirds, hundreds in number, created a steady uproar of sound, as they swooped down to the sea in search of food from their nests high up on the towering cliff faces.

Later, at age 12, somewhere between Bell Island and the little cove of St. Phillip's in Conception Bay I find myself, alone, rowing, always against the stern warnings of my dear aunt Eliza never ever to do this. I experience the roll of the sea there, and how frightening it sometimes is, and it takes my breath away. But its thrill holds me fast and enthrals me, the excitement holds me to it, and I cannot break away from the connection. Perhaps it is the life beneath the surface I have sometimes seen that frightens me. I have sometimes felt it unseen and it seems even more terrifying now; beneath the bottom of the boat it slides, and I see it later, enormous, as it rises to inspect me for just an instant, before it descends again into a more comfortable zone. I do not know what it is that I see; it could be a basking shark, if so, that's good, because the fishermen tell me that it is harmless. And the pilot whales are harmless too, unless they come too close and accidentally capsize the tiny punt that I'm commanding. I wish now my mother or somebody else had taught me how to swim. What am I doing here anyway? Oh yes! I remember now. I'm chasing after the older boys I admire so much. They always come out here jigging for fish, and I want to join them. When they see me they shout out to me.

"What're ya doin' out 'dere alone in dat boat? Your aunt Liza's goin' to be some cross wit us, if she finds out 'bout dis bye. She'll trim yer ass fer ya if she finds out 'bout dis bye, I'll tell ya dat. Let dere be no mistake 'bout it. Ya'd better be some careful in dat boat dere and not turn 'er over, fer Christ sake ."
"An' don't tear de arse out of 'er on dat sinker goin' back to de beach eder me sonny bye"!

Breathin' Down Water

When I was 7, my cousin Will was drowned. He was a good swimmer they say, but he still died that way, out there in the Bay. There was a big gash on his forehead when they found him. Everyone feels sure he must have been unconscious when he hit the water. He was an iron ore miner on Bell Island. Steady work with steady pay, sometimes dangerous, but when the fishing was slow, or if you wanted to try your hand at something else, then that was one way to do it. His older brother Jim had already been doing it for several years, to save up enough to get married to Lucy. He would lose two fingers in the mines.

It is night-time during a November snow storm, and Will is a passenger on the *Garland*, just a few minutes out from the pier on Bell Island. The *Golden Dawn*, the other ferry, left St. Phillip's 20 minutes before and has almost reached the pier when they strike. The *Garland* has a lead keel and quickly begins to sink. Perhaps Will strikes out for the shore, even though it is about 200 metres off. He is a good strong swimmer and only 27. We never know for sure. Two of his workmates and neighbours on board with him that night cannot swim. One of these men, Jack Quilty, I knew well and many years later he tells me how he manages to save himself although he can't swim. He tells how as they begin to sink and the water rises up around his legs he sits on the *Garland's* guard railing and lets himself float away, with his heavy overcoat spread open around him and a big sack of hard bread tucked under an arm. In the water he soon locates his friend Bob Lawlor, another non-swimmer who is supporting himself with a barrel and a hatch cover. Together, while shouting, singing, and praying, the two keep themselves afloat by holding each other's hands across the barrel until they are rescued. Bob's son Vince tells me years later that his father had a vision of the Blessed Virgin Mary during the night. She appeared as if standing just above the surface of the water with the Infant Jesus in her arms. Their cries for help were heard by people on the pier and, since this was war time and as several large ocean-going iron ore carriers had already been torpedoed, even while standing at the pier itself, many rescue vessels were soon on the scene of the collision. The search for survivors continued throughout the night and all the next day as well but only 6 or 7 out of over 20 on board the *Garland* were found alive. The *Golden Dawn* safely reached the pier. Two days later, Cousin Will's body was hooked with a jigger, and he is brought up.

My Cousin Will

I'll sing you a song, my friend,
About my cousin Willie's end,
And sadly do I say that yet I remember him well.
He was an iron miner when,
His fishin' got slow but then,
They've left it up to me his story to tell.

Islands of ice and snow ,
Stand like a gunner's row,
Twenty miles from nowhere, where they'd rather not go.
From all around they came, on ferries that have no name,
And lie forgotten now where nobody knows.

November winds they came,
Brought on their aches and pains,
Little did they know asleep in their cabins below,
Two ferries there they lay, upon each other's right of way,
And all too late they heard their cold whistles blow.

Now Willie could swim quite well,
Quite the best I've heard them tell,
No one worried much about our Willie that way,
But on that night he cried, as his earthly engine died,
And to the bottom down, went Willie that day.

When all is said and done,
When sometimes my fishing's done,
When I think this business has all but faded away,
There on an Autumn eve, from my other self take leave,
I think about our Willie, asleep in the bay.

A Voyage of Discovery

When I was 11, my father took me on a fabulous journey of discovery. We travelled on the Newfoundland coastal steamer *SS Northern Ranger* around the island, first northward from the capital St. John's to Battle Harbour, Labrador, then down its west coast to Corner Brook. The trip lasted several weeks and included dozens of ports of call along the way, where I witnessed a way of life since disappeared, still being practised as it had been for a couple of centuries, hard, but joyful and complete. We went to St. Anthony, White Bay, high up on the northern peninsula's north shore where Sir Wilfred Grenfell decided to establish his medical mission to the outports and aboriginal people. I saw my first Inuit there. He was dressed in native attire and looked both scary and attractive to me because he was carrying a harpoon. It was early August but he was wearing a sealskin suit and mukluks. Later, I saw many others, including women and children, some of whom were patients in the hospital there while the rest were visiting relatives or purchasing or bartering goods.

As we cross the Strait of Belle Isle to Labrador, the great ancient sea god, Father Neptune, comes. He terrifies everybody, especially the women and children, and even 11-year old boys look to find a hiding place to escape him. This monster-god I flee to escape, to run anywhere from, anywhere in the ship- the dark, smelly closets in its bowels, the cold, wet, still covered life boats up on the deck...... Thank God I'm not the only one fleeing from him, most of the women are too, and the children...... Then I notice he has helpers! Crewmen help him, and you never know who they are who'll do this. They catch us. They pick us off, one by one. Oh God, I'm really terrified. I don't think there'll be any escape. In this nightmare Father Neptune and his cohorts come steadily on, a relentless terror, inexorably advancing like a Roman legion, nothing on that ship and nothing in this life can dissuade them. Soon, all those he wishes to take with him are captured. Then in the largest salon, they are given the 'ritualistic shave' to show they've crossed the Strait.

Everywhere the *Ranger* stops there are always great throngs of people waiting for us on the wharves. This is clearly a major social event for them. The out-port VIPs are welcomed on board where they engage in gossipy conversation, games of cards and a few drinks with crew or passengers. These are mainly the merchant class and local clergy. Sometimes the medical doctor on board is summoned to attend an out-port resident's distress, which commonly is relieved by a tooth extraction. It is a society where the schoolteacher holds a position of importance, not financial as much as moral and instructional. They were a source of information from and about the outside world. During these hours the wharf remains full of people, especially children, who seem just delighted to show off for the passengers, and perhaps if they're lucky, to collect a souvenir or two. We on board are just as caught up by the activities of those on the wharf as they are with us. I go ashore for a walk sometimes. The harbours are full of schooners and fishing boats and punts. There is the smell of fish everywhere; fresh fish, salt fish, cooking fish and rotting fish. They are unloading the cod, splitting, cleaning, salting and laying them out to dry on platforms; these fish "flakes" are everywhere.

Out-port girls are very flirtatious and bold. They obviously are very keen on striking up a friendship - or more- even with a 11-year-old 'green', supposedly sophisticated townie. Probably all the better, in their eyes. There are many come-on greetings by 15 or 16-year-old comely lasses.

"Hello me duck, how are ya? From St.Jan's are ya bye? D'ya want to go fer a walk up de hill dere? We kin pick us a good feed of herts up dere bye, n' maybe som'tin else too"!

"Bye, yer some cute, you is, I bet ya knows dat, don't ya me duckie"?

There are many such lost opportunities for me in the out-ports during that trip due to an inhibiting inner shyness and hesitation, that always descends on me at just the wrong moment, and leads me away from an examination of the merits of blueberry picking. I am not a heroic figure at those times! However, it is on this wonderful coming-of-age vacation and perhaps in no small measure due to the groundbreaking work of the local girls in this department that I begin to feel the stirring of Mother Nature herself.

St. John's Jail

Come all ye young sailors both far and from near
And a tale I'll relate if you lend me an ear;
Concerning the day when my luck did me fail
And it brought me to languish in St. John's jail.

I spent all my time on the Blue Anchor Line
Since first I left home for the sea;
In this prison caught fast now I find myself cast
A victim of cruel circumstances you see.

For a judge did condemn me to my new prison home,
When first on his shore I did home;
And a sad misadventure did take me in tow
Hard bread and cold water that's all now I know.

My prison lies here near a deep lonely pond
Where the loon comes each evening at tea;
With a sad, lonely call as it flies o'er the wall,
Leaving dark, ghostly shadows my sole company.

I've no wings like the loon o'er the walls there to fly,
Fly away to my Waterford home;
Just a poor sailor's plight I'm confined here tonight
Far away from the home that I'll see never more..........

Hoist Your Sails and Run

On October 11, 1942, my mother Ita, sister Maureen, and I leave St. John's on the Newfoundland train, the *"Bullet",* bound for Port aux Basques. It is an enjoyable train ride for us in our compartment, with plenty of music and singing of songs and story telling along the way. Maureen and I get lots of coal cinders in our eyes while standing between the cars, looking ahead to where the engine is spewing out its waste of spent hot steam and coarse dry cinders. Our ultimate destination is Boston, where we will spend one year. I am seven, my sister nine.

I now think my mother was going to Boston to continue an affair she was having with an American, an ex-boarder who had stayed with us in St. John's in 1941-1942. At the time the Americans were there building a large military base. This is why we joined the *SS Caribou* to cross the gulf in the Cabot Strait. It is wartime; this is not a very safe place to be.

The cabin of the *Caribou* is dark and we speak in whispers. My mother is telling us that we must be very quiet and not turn the lights on. I hear another older woman there who is trying to muffle her crying in the darkness. My mother tries to calm her but she ends up scolding. We feel the fear all around us. There is a commotion in the passageway and a knocking at the door.

" Ita, are you all ready? Come along now! We must all attend the lifeboat drill. Take the children and their life-vests, you must all put them on! Come along right now"!

We all rush around in the darkness, mother gropes and fumbles to attach our vests. We're not crying but we sense an awful dread and fear among many of the passengers. There are also military personnel on board. I saw them earlier in the lounge, smoking and drinking as soon as the ship left port. My mother was laughing and joking with them then. Now they help to calm and reassure us and the other civilian passengers. We assemble around our lifeboat wearing our heavy coats and life-vests as a ship's mate calls out the names and lifeboat numbers. It is cold, windy and dark out there on the exposed deck. I'm not sure if this is an adventure I should be enjoying or something more sinister.

"Christopher, Ita, Maureen, John. Lifeboat number three!
In case we have to abandon ship you will come and stand here at this station, at this lifeboat. There will be crewmen here to help you. Do you understand? Is that OK then?"
"Yes, all right, I understand. You children, stay here with me! Don't wander off. Do you hear me"?

Later, we are back in our rooms. I hear the other woman crying and moaning in the night. I hear my mother too, fretting over us and attempting to calm the woman.
"Don't worry, Mrs. Skinner! We'll be all right. Nothing's going to happen to us"!

Nothing does. The *Caribou* reaches North Sydney safely. We escape the war monster that hides there in the sea, that lies waiting patiently for the *Caribou* the following night like a giant hungry sea animal.

There is no hiding the news of the catastrophe from us children. I imagine myself back in our cabin. I know its darkness, its silences, the steady humming of the engines. I can hear the muffled sounds, the hushed voices in quiet conversation, the scolding for annoyances, the calming reassurances. Then, the explosion of torpedo against hull; then yet another louder, more frightening, of boilers blowing apart. Only a few minutes remain for the senses to feel everything, to experience all the confusion and terror. The frantic fumbling with clothes and life vests, groping in the darkness along the flooding passageways, stumbling and struggling up the stairs, the slipping and sliding along precariously sloping decks. The desperate attempts being made to find a safe way off the listing sinking ship. The indescribable chaos that circles around each person, a separate whirlpool of water and wild panic, that rushes in everywhere. The searching for missing children or other family members, the confusion anxiety and tension in seeking each other out. I see one frenzy of terror follow another. A nightmare with no waking end. Broken lifeboats and rafts litter the decks. In four minutes she's gone.

In the water a few overcrowded lifeboats are afloat. There are upturned lifeboats bearing maybe twenty people and as the survivors cling to ropes there, they are one by one washed away by the sea at night. A 15-month old child is one of 15 children on board that night, and the only one of the 15 to survive the torpedoing. He somehow gets lost in the dark and sea on three different occasions but miraculously is rescued each time.

On October 13 at 7 p.m., the *SS Caribou* under Capt. Taverner a man with forty years experience left North Sydney, Cape Breton, for Port aux Basques, Newfoundland. The SS Caribou was a 2,500 tonne vessel that also saw service as a seal hunter in the springtime because of her special reinforced bows. She was escorted across the strait by a single-stack minesweeper, *HMCS*

Grandmere, which was not equipped with radar. Both boats were sailing blind at 10.5 knots when she was attacked by *U-69* under the command of Capt. Graf. He sunk her using one torpedo, forty miles from her destination. Graf wrote "On a calm night, with good visibility and weak Aurora Borealis..........she lurched down to her guard-rails with a heavy list ".

U-69 foiled *Grandmere's* attempt at ramming with a full- power emergency dive. However, four months later, northeast of Newfoundland, she would be rammed and sunk by the British destroyer *HMS Viscount*, losing all 46 hands.

In addition to the 73 civilians on board the *Caribou* were 118 military personnel, the reason used by the Germans for the attack. There was much written at the time about the courage and stamina of the *Caribou* survivors, who numbered 101, and the human dignity of those who succumbed.

Baccalieu

The winds they blow high boys, the winds they blow low,
But there's nobody left on the old Baccalieu,
And they who remember now number but few,
When the waters get rough o'er the old Baccalieu.

They brought in the salt and the coal to make dough,
She wasn't too fast and she wasn't too slow,
And one eyed Jack Quilty was Master that day,
When old Davey Jones came aboard for his pay.

The twenty year cup she was lookin' to get,
For comin' in first to the Port Nantucket,
All colours and bunting were ready to fly,
Just make for the harbour there safely to lie.

The shadows crowd sunshine from the lane,
And everything seems very much just the same,
To waken the memories of pleasures we knew,
When everyone cheered for the good Baccalieu

To finish this story the truth now I'll tell,
And hands they were lost and their fortunes as well,
And they that remember now number but few,
When the waters get rough o'er the old Baccalieu .

A Ghost in Time

When I spent my childhood vacations in the out-ports of Conception Bay, many people still believed in fairies, ghosts of all kinds, and religious, saintly or angelic occurrences. This could be a good thing or bad, depending on the time and place of the happening. My mother believed in their reality and spent her growing up years, as well as her adulthood, mostly in terror of the night, and of death, dying, the souls of all the dead, God, and judgement day. So, this life was not to be an easy ride, my sister and I soon discovered. She got this way because she always accompanied her own mother attending to the dead in the out-port. One of grand-mother Laurie's tasks was to lay out the dead shortly after they died and her daughter Ita, just a child, would always go with her on these ghostly rounds. Grandmother herself was afraid of nothing, living or dead. She came from Fogo in Notre Dame Bay and had been exposed to the hardest of pioneer experiences in that remote and unforgiving place in the 1860's. Their house in Conception Bay, perched on a high hill that overlooked the water, was only 200 feet from the top of the cliff, which fell away directly to the rocky pebble beach below.

This is where the pirates came ashore quite regularly. Some were famous, and they had come to this safe and lonely place to bury their treasure. Once, Uncle James was run off by a band of them wielding cutlasses when he came upon them by accident as they were digging a pit in the ground. Another time, he saw a headless horseman riding across a burnt-over forest area. Although it was foggy, and the figure was without a head, he was again somehow chased off by this spectre too. Ghouls and monsters were commonly seen along the narrow road that ran through the place.

I saw old Mrs. Neary's ghost when I was 12. One night I was trying to fall asleep in the very bed where she had recently succumbed when she came to me. She wore her old black shawl about her head and walked back and forth by the side of the bed the whole night. I clearly saw her form in the moonlight that fell across the bedroom wall. She continued to pace there the entire night, silently, without making any effort to disturb me. I lay awake for the duration but could make no move to leave the room or even rise from the bed for I was too consumed with fear to make any attempt to flee. To escape her tormenting presence I often turned my back on her and pressed my face to the wall that ran along the side of the bed. But each time I lay again on my back I saw that the wretched form was still there, wandering in the gloom. Finally the dawn came filling the room, leaking through delicate lace curtains and banishing the spirit. When I saw that I was released, I quickly rose from my prison on the bed and bolted from the confines of the room. Running all the way, I was breathless when I reached my Aunt Liza's house, and pounded on the door to be admitted. Even though the hour was curiously early to be arriving there and under such strange circumstances, no one queried this or commented. I took it to mean that they knew about the haunting of the old lady.

I was told about the tin whistles blowin' down in Vessel's Hole by my uncle Mike when I was 13. His wife was Julia, Aunt Liza's sister, and they had, in addition to eleven other children, a very beautiful statuesque daughter, Helen, then twenty-three, to whom I had a very strong attraction. Just down from their house and the narrow road that ran through the place, the flatness of the land suddenly fell away. Along the face of the steep cliff, rooted and uprooted trees clung precariously. Below lay the rocky shoreline, a rough place where occasionally a solitary fisherman might attempt to build a stage or attach a flake upon the boulders that littered that inhospitable site. Even more daunting were the difficulties in finding a decent place to land a skiff or punt and establish a trail up over the rock-face and peat bog to the top, 100 feet above.

Among the numerous indentations that took small bites from the land along the shore there was vessel's hole. A narrow channel, only 150 feet long, it was held in place by steep walls of stone, thirty or forty feet high. The legend of the blowin' whistles was born here almost a hundred years before Uncle Mike's birth in 1880. A small coastal schooner bound for St. Phillip's that lay nearby, was unfortunately caught there in a furious November storm, a storm with huge seas and breakers sweeping over the land. All hands on board, including a family with three small children, were lost. All the bodies were recovered and buried close by; one group in the Anglican church cemetery in St. Phillip's and the other in a tiny graveyard in Horse Cove that lay just behind the one-room school. The legend says that you can still hear on that date in November, the sound of a tin whistle blowin' just as it did on that fateful night those many long years before.

To test the power of the legend Uncle Mike brought me down to the cliff edge one dark night in November and sure enough, there could be no mistaking it. There it was, coming out of the sea, claiming the night for itself, like the sound of the sea, mixing with the winds as they swirled around us, as we huddled together upon the mountain cliff. A pitiful and sad mournful wailing, it came out over the land and sea, as if building a monument to the dead in the waters, a living testimony of lives lived before we came this way.

Whales

The winds blow low out across the bay
The waters high along about May
There're black-eyed Susans back on shore,
But you won't find whales out here any more.

The Captain's cursin' out some song,
He's been away from home too long,
And all the rum now he's glad that he stored,
' cause he can't find whales out here anymore.

And still he sails across the ocean dreamin' through his tears,
He'd taken almost twenty thousand back across the years,

The shadows roll out across the sea,

There's nothing there and there'll never be,

The old man lies dreamin' behind his door,

'cause he can't find whales out here anymore.

And he really knows how it used to be

How you'd hear them pushin' right down thru the sea,

Let's both have a drink now but I'd better pour,

'cause you won't find whales out here anymore.

And still he sails across the ocean, dreamin' through his tears,
He'd taken almost twenty thousand back across the years.

23

Author on beach in Whale Cove, Hudson Bay - 1962

Part Two: The Harp Seal Hunt Aboard MV THeron

Hillary, Maru, and Me

All this happened more than 40 years ago now and before memory completely fails me I am persuaded by some muse to put it down as best I can. I have heard it said that when fact becomes legend, print the legend. I believe, however, that I am still at a point where what follows can be regarded as factual and where myths have yet to intrude.

I first came on board the *MV Theron* the last week of February, 1962. She was tied up at a Dartmouth, Nova Scotia pier and was expected to sail within a few days for "*the front*" off Newfoundland's' north-east coast in search of harp seals. I think that by that time almost all other hands had already come aboard. My workmate for this, my first voyage "to the ice", for the *Fisheries Research Board of Canada* was Danny Welch, an Englishman. We had both travelled down to Halifax together from Montreal (where we had been working for *FRB's Arctic Unit*) and had settled in on board the same day. For this particular trip to the ice, *Theron* had about sixty Newfoundland sealers signed on, in addition to six Nova Scotian deckhands and the ship's Norwegian officers, who included the captain and chief engineer.

We were warmly welcomed on board by the officers and crew that day. The jovial, heavy-set, chain-smoking chief engineer still stands out in my mind. Quiet-spoken and with an easygoing sense of humour he had a way of understating even the most serious and difficult problems that were to come our way during the voyage.

The *MV Theron*, built in Norway in the early 1950's, was still at that time regarded as state-of-the-art for conducting research in polar ice. Constructed specifically to work in this type of environment she had extremely good manoeuvrability, a reinforced steel hull, and had been designed to ride on top of the ice and crush it with her weight as she advanced through it. She was about one thousand tonnes in weight and about two hundred feet in length.

I should explain here that the *Theron* had already made quite a reputation for herself and her Norwegian crew back in 1956, while serving as HQ for the *Advance British Expeditionary Team* to the Antarctic, and serving as the base of operations for such notables as Edmund Hillary (later Sir Edmund) and Vivian Fuchs. As it was, the same Captain and officers were still with the *Theron* in 1962 as had been with her back in 1956. I certainly regarded this as a stroke of luck, for, in addition to hearing of many personal anecdotes about Sir Edmund, I actually got to use the same cabin and bunk that had been Hillary's only five years earlier. As an aside, perhaps I should mention here that years later, around 1973 or 1974, Hillary passed through Toronto, Ontario, where I happened to be working at the time. He was on a promotional tour representing some outdoor and camping equipment that was being sponsored by the T. Eaton Company Ltd. I called him at his hotel to introduce myself and to tell him of my connection with him by way of the *Theron.* I also spoke with his wife that day who was later to tragically die in an air crash in Nepal.

Maru, the Captain, struck me as a shy and formal person, like someone from another time and place, as indeed he was. I liked him and he me, so we got along well, without any serious conflicts occurring to mar our relationship during the weeks and months we worked together. That afternoon, Maru showed Welch and me to our cabin up on the bridge deck, next to the officer's saloon. He and the chief had their cabins along this same short corridor. Curiously, opposite our cabin, there was another cabin, locked and unoccupied. I was quite amazed, but agreeably so, to discover that it held dozens of cases of beer and spirits, when Maru later showed us around the area. It was indeed an impressively stocked liquor cabinet to be enjoyed by so few.

I had already worked at the *FRB Arctic Unit* station in Montreal for a few months with Welch, so he wasn't an entirely unknown quantity to me. He was a nice enough fellow, if somewhat remote and aloof. For this reason he sometimes turned people off unwittingly, and didn't draw them to him easily. I wasn't exactly thrilled by the idea of having to spend several months sharing the same small cabin with him (quite possibly he felt the same about me), but I had reconciled myself to the idea nevertheless, as being part of the job. Besides, I knew him to be a technically resourceful and reliable person, who could be depended upon to get a job done in an emergency. Since my childhood days, I had heard and read about famous Newfoundland sealing disasters and knew that it still could be a dangerous undertaking. More precisely, the great *Newfoundland* disaster of 1912 came to mind, when more than a 100 men from that vessel (including my Uncle Dick), became lost on the ice during a terrible blizzard and 78 froze to death. A sense of excitement and adventure existed for me at the time, however, and overcame any misgivings I might have, so that when this job offer came along, I eagerly accepted it.

Welch was not quite of average stature, being shorter and slighter. He had a full beard, which gave him the appearance of Peter Freuchen the great Arctic explorer, whose picture I had seen in a biography when he was a young man. Welch had small penetrating eyes. One felt upon meeting him that here was a determined individual, but one without much of a sense of humour. He was already something of a world traveller, and had worked in numerous places and in various capacities: a sort of jack of all trades. He could pass at anything and everything, from carpentry and photography, to electrical circuits. He was also at that time keenly interested in Eastern philosophies and mysticism, a common dalliance among young people during the 1960's. His principal interest in me, I remember, was the fact that I played the guitar and sang folk songs (another popular activity at the time). Also, I came from a part of North America that couldn't be considered mainstream and might even have been thought of as an interesting place by him, for that very reason.

Within a few days I had established good relations with all the officers and crew. The Norwegians and Nova Scotians on the *Theron* were all basically down-to-earth and easygoing men, who found it difficult to relate to my companion Welch, because of his esoteric interests. In retrospect, I think that perhaps he was simply too complicated psychologically for most of us to appreciate.

The night before sailing I invited several of my Halifax friends to come aboard for a few drinks, and to have a look around. I showed them through the engine room, where the chief graciously explained the workings, then through the forecastle where we had a chat with some of the sealers. Here we saw that they already had a batch of home brew going, and naturally, we were invited to sample it, but we thought that it was not yet quite ready. Later on we had a few drinks from our own well- stocked *"liquor cabinet"*, and shared in singing some songs in the lounge, before saying our good-byes. The next afternoon under overcast skies and in a light snowfall we cast off our mooring lines and set out. As we sailed out of Halifax I recognised Point Pleasant Park off to starboard, a favourite haunt of mine. Very soon the land was left behind and the *Theron* headed into the North Atlantic. So, I thought to myself, here I am on my way to the seal hunt aboard a Norwegian vessel, and just a few months after being a pipe salesman at the Eaton's downtown store in Montreal. What luck!

Our seal hunting begins

We sailed northeast to a position off Cape Race, Newfoundland, then north along the Newfoundland coast until we encountered the heavy Arctic ice pack in the Notre Dame Bay area. We then cruised along the floe edge taking on board scattered seals, mainly adult animals, but a few younger ones as well. This activity continued for several days but we saw no large concentration of animals or any indication of the main herd. I saw there, a sealer engaged in a struggle to kill a large male hood seal, about 8 ft. in length. It had its air bubble fully inflated, which covered the forehead and the face area for protection while fighting. In this way the head was quite well shielded from the blows that the sealer was attempting to score, in order to subdue him. The sealer kept attacking the head with blows from his long sturdy wooden gaff, and the large heavy iron hook, attached to the end of his tow rope, hoping to land a knockout blow. It was a long and difficult fight, but finally the sealer succeeded in killing it. He then towed the carcass to the ship and we brought it on board. It was a beautiful specimen, known in Newfoundland as a blue-back because of its lovely, silvery blue-black sheen. Its pelt was worth considerably more in cash value, than that of the harp seal, and for this reason it was sought out especially, if hunters thought that it was in the area. However it was only rarely seen around there, being more commonly found in the Greenland Sea. But the *Theron's* business was to hunt the harp seal and its young the prized white-coats, which brought good prices for their very valuable and beautiful pelts.

I had been provided with a movie camera by the *National Film Board of Canada,* with which I hoped to capture activities on board the ship, and record aspects of the hunt itself. For example, I recorded on film, two ways in which fresh drinking water was brought on board. In one, blocks of ice were cut directly from the rafted ice of the ice floe, passed along man to man, and finally placed directly into the ship's holding tanks. Using the other method, water was pumped directly aboard into the tanks, from the large pools of fresh water that often accumulated on the ice pans, from either, melting snow and ice, or, from rainfall. In this way we filled our tanks, as we went along, or whenever it was necessary or opportune to do so.

I also shot some film of the sealer's living conditions on board. They were situated in the ship's forecastle, and I had been given a look around their quarters shortly after coming on board, that first day. At that time, I had spoken to several of them, and they had seemed happy enough with the set-up there, and everyone was looking ahead eagerly to the hunt. Bunk beds lined both sides of the ship's hull, as well as the bulkheads, forward, along each side of a narrow passageway, two and sometimes three deep. It had seemed to me then, that they were a bit squeezed for space. Although they would be living in such crowded conditions, I heard no complaining, only good-natured joking about the hunt that lay ahead. There was a lot of talk about how overweight and out of shape they were, and how they'd have to work it off, when the hard work of the seal hunt really began. Even though the sea wasn't particularly rough on that day, it seemed to me as I stood there in the forecastle, that the steady constant grinding and bumping of the ship against waves and swell created quite a racket, and made it difficult to stand without supporting myself against a bulkhead. This small, cramped, uncomfortable space, would be home for them for the next several months.

When there was a break in the action from the actual hunt itself, for example, when we were sailing in open water from one location to another, or when we were stuck in the ice in a place far removed from the seals, we often gathered in the small lounge for a few drinks and a chat. Maru or the chief would then launch forth with fascinating accounts of past voyages to Antarctica or elsewhere, and tell of strange encounters they'd had in remote parts of South America or the Far East. I still remember tales of bizarre adventures that they'd had in Indonesia. During these social occasions, I managed to learn a little Norwegian and even a few of their folk songs, which we then all sang heartily after a few rums. These songs never failed to bring on a few tears of nostalgia afterwards, from the Norwegians gathered there. I also remember learning to sing in Norwegian two contemporary songs of the day: "*Where have all the flowers gone"*, and "*Everyone loves Saturday night*". Years later, I tried singing these two songs at a party in Stockholm one night, which brought forth great hoots of laughter. I assumed it was because of my accent or pronunciation, but then again maybe it wasn't, for the Swedes tend to react in a bemused way to all things Norwegian, and indeed are inclined to regard them in a way, as their inferiors. In this respect, it is similar to the way in which Newfoundlanders are regarded, by many "*mainlanders*" in Canada.

We had not been long in the floe ice before seeing late one evening, first the silhouette of one ship, then a second, and then yet another, coming up over the horizon from the East. Finally a long line of 17 ships could be made out, in the dim light of a darkening evening sky, entering the pack ice. These were the European-based seal hunters, from Norway mainly, but others from Germany and the USSR. That year, 1962, Canada had maybe 6 ships out of St. John's, Newfoundland, and 4 out of Halifax, Nova Scotia. There were as well, a couple of smaller vessels from the Newfoundland out-ports. The seal hunt had begun to wind down somewhat that year, due to weakening European markets, and poor prices. Also, a strong outcry against the seal hunt had begun to be heard in recent years, from Europe, and more *"humane ways"* of killing the white-coats were being tried out under the supervision of Fisheries Department inspectors. They were then trying out a new rope-and-hook method to replace the old Newfoundland gaff method, thinking it was a more efficient and humane way of to kill the white-coat pups. But this was never convincingly demonstrated to me, to be the case.

The individual hunters were being instructed (and encouraged), to be more thorough when killing the pups. More precisely, they were told to give the pup a good solid blow, or several if need be, to the skull, to make sure that the pup was fully unconscious, before attempting to skin it. It was being claimed at the time, that large numbers of pups were suffering unnecessarily, because of the careless and insensitive killing techniques being employed by many seal hunters (and probably with some justification). It is true, that sometimes live and fully conscious pups were hideously skinned. From conversations I had then, I know that large numbers of sealers felt very badly about the way in which some hunters killed the white-coats. Nevertheless, it is hard to imagine that even under the most humane circumstances, that the spectacle of the seal hunt could be seen as anything but grim and repellent, in the eyes of most neutral observers.

I would like to relate a cautionary tale here of the extremes to which people will go in order to establish or maintain social relations. One night several other Norwegian sealing ships assembled close by the *Theron*. I soon discovered that they were skippered by brothers of our own Maru, and that seal hunting was a family tradition with them, something that went back across several centuries, originating from a small village in the north of Norway, called Olsen. That night, several people came over to the *Theron* across fifty or more yards of heaving ice, from each of the other ships. A long evening of socialising and drinking followed, with lots of animated talk, interspersed with the singing of many songs. I enjoyed the evening's activities and got to meet all our visitors.

As well as exchanging the family gossip and the latest news from Norway, opinions were offered, and information given about that year's ice conditions, weather, and seal herd locations (since they were all family). Of course, as the night wore on, they all became increasingly, more tipsy, and by the time it was decided to call it a night, most of them were already quite a bit under the weather. Nevertheless, they all proceeded to climb over the *Theron's* rail and down the wooden boarding ladders, and on to the ice... and then attempt to return to their own vessels. This of course was by now, something of a hazardous undertaking. For now, in addition to their quite intoxicated state, a fearful swell had come up during the evening, opening up numerous wide and dangerous leads in the ice between the ships, and making the return journey across the ice pans a very risky business for them. I watched in fascination to see how events would unfold. Luckily however for all concerned, help was at hand. Before they'd taken many faltering, slipping and sliding steps, and only fallen down once or twice (with nobody actually falling into the ocean), they were all quickly rescued by the various ships' stewards, and other crew, who sprang over their vessels' sides, to collect them and carry them off home safely. During this entire misadventure, the ships had kept their powerful searchlights on to help bring about a successful outcome, while several of us on the deck sang a chorus of "*Show me the way to go home*". I recall thinking at the time that all this seemed to have a well rehearsed feel to it, as if the players there on the ice, had acted out their roles many times before.

It was shortly after this great social event, that we came upon a huge herd of seals, hauled out on the ice. By this time i.e. late March, all the pups were born, and most would be now around a month old. Soon they would be able to fend for themselves and go into the water in search of food. By this time, the beautiful white coat was beginning to moult as well, and had now a patchy appearance. This new look of theirs, resulted in their acquiring a new name during this period: they were now known locally as "*raggedy jackets*".

The adult seals were now coming into the peak of their mating season. This would be their last big social event of the year, following which the great herds would disperse and return to the North again, in small family units. I observed them with my binoculars as we approached through heavy ice. It was quite hard going for the *Theron* to make much progress, but we advanced by punching through whatever leads Maru could find in the ice. I had to admire the man's patience and endurance, for he stood, often for hours on end, up in the "barrel" i.e. crow's nest, exposed to the elements in the bitter cold winds; fifty or sixty feet. up on the main mast, directing operations from there. I myself had made the trip up to the "barrel" only once, and then when the *Theron* was still at the dock in Dartmouth.

Again I tried some filming of the *Theron*'s approach, up to within a mile or so of the herd. Maru cut the engines when we were about 200 to 300 yards from them. As it was late evening, and too late to begin hunting, we spent the night there, held firm in the embrace of the heavy arctic ice floe. Very early the next morning, our first big kill of seals began, when our " gunners", four or five men, went over the side and out onto the ice, and began shooting adult animals. Some attempt was made to avoid the killing of breeding females, if they could be identified as such, but I know that this could not be done very successfully. The whole day was spent shooting seals. As there were tens of thousands of them in the herd here, it was almost as easy as shooting fish in a barrel. Our gunners cut an immense swath through the herd while the *"swillers"*, that is, the skinners who were the main body of the sealers, came behind skinning the dead and dying animals. Smaller groups of men built up large mounds of seal pelts on the ice pans, marked with the *Theron's* distinctive flags, to be picked up later on.

This method of flag marking was employed by the different mercantile companies engaged in the seal hunt, so that there would be no confusion, or squabbling, over the various piles of pelts scattered about the ice. It was a tradition that went back to the early days of sealing in Newfoundland. As a large herd consisted of several hundred thousand animals, and could be scattered over a huge ice surface, it was a given that ships from many different countries, not to mention those from the St. John's companies, would all be there somewhere "in the fat". If you were to take a walk across such an ice floe, you could be sure to come upon large numbers of these mounds of pelts, marked by the flags of the various foreign countries, and local companies. Our crew worked all day, and late into the night, picking up *Theron* pelts and stowing them in her holds. As every pelt was counted as it was stowed, we knew that 1400 adult harp seals had been shot that day, by her gunners.

Perils on the ice

One day, we heard over the ship's radio that another Norwegian vessel out of Halifax, was stuck in the heavy ice and unable to break free. We also learned that she had not been reinforced to work in the ice, and was therefore in danger of being crushed and foundering. We proceeded in the company of several other vessels, to where she was stuck, and lay to, near by. With some other people I walked across the ice, to where she was tightly held, motionless and still, in order to inspect her more closely. By now of course she had been abandoned, and many personal effects, as well as various kinds of ship's apparatus and equipment could be seen lying around on the ice, near her. I took a quick look through her (we had time for that), and noticed that she had been gutted of practically everything that could be removed. It was strangely eerie and very quiet within her, the only sounds being those of the ice squeezing, and pressing against her hull, in an ever-tighter grip. We left her like this, and shortly afterwards she caved in, and sunk. I heard that she hadn't many pelts stowed aboard, but I saw that some had been removed and were piled on the ice nearby. Because there had been gossip about her not being a sound vessel, and one that shouldn't have been at the ice hunting seals in the first place, more malicious gossip soon surfaced about a deliberate sabotage by the owners, or on their behalf, by the captain, to collect the insurance on her. Her captain was a most memorable odd little man, of middle age, scruffy and elfish in appearance. It seemed that he might have been dropped into our midst from another century, like some ancient Scandinavian troll.

Getting around on the ice and working on it, could be at all times perilous, especially for the first-time-to–the-ice greenhorns like Welch and myself. Old hands were willing to give advise of course, on ways to recognise dangerous ice conditions and how and when to avoid specific areas on the ice. They also gave us important information on the ice leads, the crevasses running helter-skelter all over the ice floes, each one of them a potential trap for the unwary. The layout of these leads, would determine the safest routes to use when crossing the ice pans to approach seals or to return to the ship. We were also told to use large formations of ice, called rafted ice, as areas for rest and protection from the elements. These strange formations some in appearance like ice fortresses, were formed by the ocean currents and swells thrown up during violent storms. On many occasions in the past they had been used by lost or temporarily marooned sealers as effective natural wind breaks which kept them alive by providing them with the time needed for a safe rescue.

Hunting seals on the ice was dangerous. It was easy for men to become separated from their ship and become lost on the ice, especially so in the event of a sudden snow storm. One could easily fall into the sea from an ice pan by accident, or when using the large heavy two-by-four wooden frames hanging over the ship's side that served as ladders for exiting and boarding the ship. A hapless sealer might step suddenly into a snow covered and hidden crevasse in the ice (as I did on several occasions) and get an unexpected icy dunking, or even drown. Small groups of isolated men trapped and stranded on small ice pans broken off from the main ice floe had been known to perish from exposure, when rescue was not quick. While I was on the *Theron,* I heard that a sealer had lost his life while attempting to jump to the vessel's boarding ladders, from the ice floe below. As the ship passed through the ice near him, he accidentally fell into the sea between the ship's hull and the wooden frames, in making his leap from the ice floe to the ladder. Traditionally, these sealing ships never stopped to let just a few men off or to pick them up again, for example, if they were picking up just scattered seals. They would only make a complete stop if the animals were plentiful, and when a large number of the ship's company had to be sent over the side to hunt. If only three or four men were on the ice to be picked up, the ship only slowed down very slightly for them. It was, therefore, a risky business to jump back on to the ladders of the moving ship, from the ice. I was forced to do this myself once or twice, and thought myself lucky to do it successfully. But there were a few close calls for me, nevertheless.

On one occasion as Welch and I were walking across the ice, we decided to take a break from our collecting chores. We chose a nearby mound of ice blocks on which to rest, and headed for their shelter. Welch, who had been leading the way, was already seated on a comfortable ice block, unpacking his lunch kit, as I approached. Suddenly, and without any indication of danger, I found myself suspended in the ocean, dangling down from the armpits. I was wedged tightly luckily, into the narrow crevasse separating two large ice pans. I had stepped into one of those dangerous snow covered hidden leads that I'd been warned about, and luckily for me, right in front of Welch who sat there resting, just about to begin his snack. There I was, frantically clawing at the ice floe around me, trying to haul myself out of the slushy gulch in the ice floe. Immediately Welch came to my rescue and grabbed me by the coat collars. He stopped me from going down into the hole any deeper, and then hauled me out onto the ice floe like he would a seal.

Another time, as Welch and I were jumping along over the ice pans, another near calamity struck. On this trip we had been forced to leap across many leads between the ice pans. Most were no more than two or three feet wide and not dangerous, although a little scary in appearance. At one lead however, after leaping across and landing on the far ledge, it suddenly broke away. I soon found myself marooned on a small rolling ball of ice, about the size of an ordinary kitchen table. I attempted to keep my balance on it and to avoid falling off as it slowly began to drift away from the main ice pan upon which Welch was standing, and who now stared incredulously at what was unfolding before his eyes. In terror I discovered that my slightest movement caused the ball of ice to react immediately, with a very steep rolling motion of its own. It was an horrific experience while it lasted, especially for a non-swimmer such as I was. Although the ball and I were only a few feet from the floe, I just couldn't steady it enough to attempt a leap back to the ice floe. Both Welch and I had our long 6 ft. wooden gaffs with us, which we often used for checking out suspicious looking places on the ice, before crossing. It was Welch's gaff that saved me! All the while that I was struggling with the ice ball he kept trying to calm me, and to build up my confidence. Finally I had the ice ball stable enough, and close enough to the main floe for a rescue attempt to be made. I was then within reach of his six-foot gaff, which he held out to me, and which I very carefully grasped. He then pulled me ever so gently towards him so that finally I was able to step safely onto the main ice floe.

Science and Industry

I had been engaged by the *FRB* as a marine mammalogist to collect biological specimens while on the hunt. The owners, The *Karlsen Shipping Company*, had offered accommodation for two and space for the storage of equipment and specimens i.e. barrels, tubs, crates, jars etc. for we intended to collect everything, from skulls to individual teeth and reproductive organs, material that would assist in evaluating the age of the animals and the impact if any, of seal hunting on their survival. The technique being employed by the *FRB* at that time to age the animals, could be described as follows: the canine teeth were extracted from the carcasses while they were still lying on the ice, where they had been killed. These teeth were then placed in glycerine-filled vials, to preserve them in a healthy condition, until they could be examined back at the laboratory. There, they were sectioned using electric saws, then ground down on lathes to a thickness where one could count the rings each contained, using binocular microscopes. It was thought at the time that there was a direct one-to-one relationship between the number of rings and the age in years, but scientists weren't entirely sure of this interpretation. We also collected stomach contents from a few animals at random, in order to see what they were eating at different times, and in different locations, during this their breeding season. Interestingly, a study publicised by University of Guelph scientists in November 1992, has shown that harp seals are not big eaters of North Atlantic cod, and therefore, cannot be considered responsible for the critical decline in the cod stocks. They examined approximately 9,200 seal stomachs, collected from the mid 1950's to the present. I would like to think that some of the material we collected then, also found its way into their study.

To further the current knowledge of harp seal reproduction, we removed and preserved large numbers of ovaries at that time as well, which were also returned to the lab for analysis. *FRB* activities were then concentrated in determining, as accurately as possible, the composition of the harp seal population, in the massive herds off the Newfoundland and Labrador coasts. Their scientists hoped to get an accurate picture of the age and sex distribution within these herds, during their migratory breeding period in March and April.

It was then becoming widely accepted that the length of the hunt should be reduced from what it was i.e. open-ended, to one of maybe only three or four weeks. Fears were already starting to surface in many quarters, that possibly it was the hunt itself that was the villain in the works, the agent responsible for the alarming reduction in herd sizes, in comparison to those of just a few decades earlier. The hunt had always been orchestrated in its planning and execution on a grand scale it is true, involving thousands of men and scores of vessels. But now, newer and more deadly technological devices from the seal's view-point, were being brought to bear on the hunt i.e. in locating the animals and then tracking them down for the kill. Modern icebreakers were now easily available and frequently used, to assist vessels get through heavy pack ice to where the animals would be found herding in vast numbers. Also, the use of helicopters was now commonplace in locating the nurseries of the white-coats, and the breeding grounds of the adults. All of this quite obviously, was making it easier to kill seals. In response to growing public criticism and the agitation of conservationists, and also as a result of several preliminary studies just completed by *FRB*, more comprehensive studies were being undertaken. In these, *FRB* scientists wanted to come up with statistical evidence that would show conclusively, one way or the other, whether hunting adversely affected harp seal populations.

Peril on board ship

I had completed a few courses in the basic medical sciences, while a student at Dalhousie University, in Halifax, and had in addition, worked for a while in that university's hospital pathology section. These experiences, taken along with the fact that I had also completed a *St. John Ambulance* first aid course, which he had somehow discovered, made me the Captain's first choice to act as the ship's medical officer the moment our first medical problem arose. The *Theron* had an excellent and fully equipped emergency medical and surgical section, as well as an impressively stocked pharmaceutical cabinet. Here, we had surgical texts, surgical instruments, first aid equipment, medical texts and instruments of all kinds. All this had been left over from the glory days of the Antarctic expedition most likely, and probably had not been used since. I hadn't been asked to look at anything more serious than a few "bad" teeth during the first six weeks out. Then, suddenly out of the blue a real medical emergency fell upon us, and one I would have to deal with no matter how reluctantly I felt about it. At the time, we were again stuck in the ice, somewhere in the Strait of Belle Isle and were unable do anything about it but drift helplessly along on the Labrador current, southward, through the Strait.

It was at this time and while we found ourselves in this awkward predicament that a young Newfoundland crewman came down with a badly inflamed and infected appendix. For assistance in dealing with this problem I immediately called on the ship to shore radio, a medical doctor stationed at the cottage hospital on Fogo Island, Notre Dame Bay, Newfoundland. We were instructed to begin treatment by administering large doses of the antibiotic *Aureomycin* to fight the infection. This treatment was continued for about a week but was unsuccessful in controlling the infection. It was apparent that the man's condition was deteriorating daily, accompanied as it was by more severe pain and higher temperatures. Our patient, a good-natured and stoical young fellow of maybe 21, had for some strange reason developed an unnatural confidence in my ability to cure him, which I found very touching, if inappropriate and misplaced. Although I was becoming more alarmed and anxious by the hour, he continued to remain in cheerful high spirits throughout the whole affair. At last, and when there was no other recourse left, we were told by the medical doctor at the cottage hospital that we would have to perform an emergency appendectomy on the patient. Even more alarming was the news that I would have to supervise it myself! Naturally, I was very reluctant to comply with this directive immediately. Indeed, I was not anxious to follow his instruction at all if I could possibly avoid it. I expressed my concerns to Maru, but he supported the doctor in every respect and was adamant that I should follow the doctor's instructions. So it happened that the Captain, the steward, and I, began to prepare ourselves and the patient, for the operation.

The steward, who up to then had attended to us in only an routine if efficient way, began suddenly to transform himself into a saviour. As we were discussing the task that lay ahead, he revealed to us that he had been a medic in the Norwegian resistance during the Second World War, had all kinds of experience in dealing with medical emergencies, and was very familiar with operating room procedures. Because he showed not the least bit of anxiety, his attitude quickly brought about a marked reduction in my own level of anxiety. Indeed, I now began to feel that the patient might even survive what we were about to do to him. Things got even better, as the steward continued to build up my confidence in his abilities, with more and more reassuring tales of his wartime successes in the operating theatre: he had dealt with bullet, bayonet and shrapnel wounds; he had sutured up incisions and wound damage. The only thing I had to do was make the incision, or, if I preferred, to show him where to made it, and he would be happy to do it. So we settled on the latter arrangement, which suited me just fine.

From the surgical text-book available I soon located the position on the lower abdomen called *MacBirney's Point*, where the incision was to be made to get at the appendix. It would lie immediately below, if everything was normal anatomically in our patient. Between the two of us we decided that we could remove the appendix successfully. Meanwhile, Maru would stand by and oversee everything. Although Maru had seemed more than a little anxious and apprehensive about the outcome earlier on, by now, the steward's marvellous reports had relieved him of all doubts. However, it was true that we hadn't very much of a idea about what we were about to do, or how we would go about doing it. Maru suggested we all have a stiff drink or two at this stage in order to celebrate our good luck in having the steward with us, and also probably to fortify ourselves. We thought this was a very good idea.

The galley table was selected to be the site of the operation, which soon brought the cook into the picture. He, too, wanted to get involved in the action but Maru blocked every move he made to get himself included on the operating room team- the galley being too small. He would let him serve as an attendant in some way though if he so desired. We now began to make our patient ready for the operation. He remained as good-natured and confident about the outcome as ever. This blind faith of his increased our own self-confidence which by now was getting a little out of hand due to the stiff drinks of Lamb's rum that Maru poured for us. And then it happened! No not the operation. In fact, just the opposite. There would be no operation after all! Miraculously, at the very instant that we were about to start the surgery, our patient was rescued from imminent danger by the opportune arrival on the scene of a Canadian government icebreaker. Quickly, he was removed from our care by a helicopter and brought to a modern hospital in Corner Brook, Newfoundland, where his appendix was successfully removed. There, he made a complete and quick recovery. A month later he rejoined the *Theron,* none the worse for wear. When we arrived back in Dartmouth, it was a pleasant surprise to find awaiting me, two letters. One was from the hospital surgeon in Corner Brook, telling me that the patient was still singing our praises many days after the operation and the other was from the owner of the company, Mr. Karlsen himself, graciously offering me a free passage on any Karlsen shipping line vessel and at any time.

I had not expected to be caught in any bad weather during our trip out seal hunting that year. I assumed we would sail without incident from Halifax to *"the front"* off the Labrador coast, in a couple of days, stay there more or less for a month, just long enough to get a good load of pelts on board and return to Halifax, with smooth sailing all the way. I was wrong!

Our getting stuck in the heavy pack ice in the Strait of Belle Isle resulted in our having to sail completely around the island of Newfoundland in order to get back again to the seal herds off the Labrador coast. From the point where we finally broke free of the ice off Newfoundland's west coast, we had to sail south into the Gulf of St. Lawrence, then east, along the south coast of the island. We passed by the French islands of St. Pierre and Miquelon, where we encountered immense fog banks, and passed among large numbers of foreign, ocean going draggers and factory ships. Finally, we steered north to the front again, after rounding Cape Race, North America's most easterly point of land, situated on Newfoundland's Avalon Peninsula. It should now take about a day to reach the front from there. The next morning, we noticed that a heavy wind had come up during the night, and the sky was beginning to cloud over. Maru told us that the weather service was calling for a heavy winter storm to hit our area sometime during the day. Sure enough, by that afternoon we were in the thick of a bad one.

It was a storm of unforgettable intensity, and an awesome experience, like something I could only remember having read about. In order not to miss any of the storm's visual fury, I settled down on one of the *Theron's* lockers, situated at the stern of the ship, and there experienced the most exciting roller coaster-like ride that I'd had in my life till then. Absolutely mountainous seas came racing up behind us, forty and fifty feet in height, lifting us up to their peaks like a toy and then letting us slide smoothly down into their troughs, over and over, hypnotically.

We had all been kept busy throughout the morning, seeing to our gear and equipment, and making sure that everything was as firmly secured as possible in anticipation of the storm. It was the cook who had to contend with the most serious difficulties. Everything under his care required his continuous attention. Regardless of all his best efforts however, pots and pans continued to fall down and roll around about him, throughout a very long day, and all the while he could be heard cursing loudly through all the noise and commotion. Even so, he still managed to keep the home fires going for us and despite everything there was always hot tea available and something good to snack on.

I had not experienced anything like it before. This storm had sent practically everybody to bed, incapacitated by sea-sickness to some degree, even those who could normally tolerate pretty foul weather. I was forced to climb into my own bunk early, too, and spent long hours suffering there. Welch was absolutely miserable and in the vilest mood I'd yet seen him in during the whole trip. His misery left him without the slightest trace of a social grace. Throughout the night I could hear the heavy seas breaking all around us, and the constant banging, and lurching of the ship as she lay to. Maru had decided to stay put for the night. By running the engines at only half speed ahead, and keeping her head into the gale, he managed to keep her more or less stationary, during the long night. This strategy minimized risk and danger to the ship, and provided a more comfortable night's rest for all on board. That night, while lying in my bunk, but too sick to do anything about it, I could hear my guitar being thrown around in the cabin locker.

The next day, in calmer seas, I ventured out of my bed to investigate and discovered the guitar smashed, probably beyond repair. It had been a nice little concert- size Gibson guitar, *"Kalamazoo"* model. My father had bought it for me new in 1948. Without a moment's hesitation I took it to the ship's rail and dropped it overboard into the ocean. I had to spend the remainder of the voyage without music, a major loss alas! It was now April and we still had only a few thousand pelts on board, and needed lots more, maybe 10 thousand more, to make it a profitable trip for everyone. We found our way back to the main herds again off Hamilton Inlet, Labrador, without encountering any more serious difficulties. Immediately, the gunners were sent over the side by the Captain to begin shooting the seals . They were quickly followed by the *"swillers"*, to skin the hundreds of slain animals that lay about.

A few weeks following our arrival there we noticed one day that the great herds we had been working on suddenly seemed to disappear, as if by magic. It is true that large numbers of animals had been taken by the combined sealing fleet, probably 200,000 or more, but there may have been well over a million in the total population. It was now May, and spring conditions were taking hold all around us. The great ice floes had ceased their southward drift, and had begun to melt quite noticeably. The young seals had been born and started swimming. The adult animals had mated again by now. The herds, following a biological instinct were dispersing and preparing for their long journey back to Arctic waters where they would spend the summer months feeding. For them, the circle was closed for another year. Although many had been lost by drowning, crushed between the ice floes, or eaten by polar bears (for many were hunting on the ice, along with us) during their first weeks after birth, many thousands of young had survived to follow their mothers and older siblings northward.

For us, too, it was time to turn the page on another season of hunting and prepare for the journey home. We had 14,000 pelts stowed below in our holds and there would be profits to be shared between the owners and Captain (full share), officers and crew (half share), and the sealers (quarter share). A feeling of excitement and anticipation filled us all as we headed for open water once again, this time for Halifax and home. It was now the middle of May, and we had been away since the end of February. We had been hunting the seals for long enough that year! Indeed, it was a strongly held opinion among many sealers including the Captain that it should not be necessary to have to continue in this way of life year after year for an entire lifetime, just for the sake of a few dollars.

Some radio and TV people were at the dockside when we tied up in Dartmouth. They had come by to shoot a few frames of film, and record a few words of the people on board the *Theron*, if any wished to say anything. Few did. Brigitte Bardot had not yet arrived on the scene to make this the celebrity event it was to soon become.

The Whalefish

We sailed aboard in Theron's crew, in the year of '61,
Put our trust in Maru brave, whose equal there was none.
So outward bound we made away, our homes we left behind,
For the place of icy waters cold, the whalefish there to find.
Caught fast we lay in the Arctic Sea , that ice we could not flee,
For 50 days and nights we roamed, that mighty fish to see.
At last we spied our mighty prize, he blew a spout so high ,
When e 'er he blew we heard the cry, go catch him now me byes.
So with our mates we then gave chase, this truth I tell today,
There from the deep and full of fight, our mighty whalefish lay.
Our deadly darts we shot away, to hook that blubbered hide,
That mighty fish went straight he down, from fright we nearly died.
He left us there in disarray, our only chance you see,
To cut our lines and leave him there, and set old whalefish free.
A'whalin' I'll not go again, on that you can be sure,
I'll stay on land and take a wife, I'll hunt whalefish no more..............

Author sitting on beluga, Whale Cove -1962

Inuit holding an arctic char and net, A Hudson Bay beach 1962

Author and Seku at whale net

A beluga whale foetus - 1963

Part Three: The North

Beluga whale collecting

Shortly after completing the seal-hunting trip aboard the *MV Theron* to the Newfoundland *"front"* and Labrador and our return to Halifax, I learned that I would be going north to assist Dr. David Sergeant on his beluga whale research. We would be working out of a newly created settlement on the north-western coast of Hudson Bay called Whale Cove, which was situated several hours by boat south of Rankin Inlet, the administrative centre for the region at that time.

It was already mid May by the time we settled things in Halifax and Dartmouth, where *Theron* was tied up. Our collections of seal teeth, stomach contents and seal skulls were transferred from the vessel to the *Fisheries Research Board* station in Halifax for delivery to the *Arctic Unit* research labs in Montreal. Depending on local ice conditions we planned on arriving in Whale Cove towards the middle of June.

As I was familiar with the Halifax area from my university days at Dalhousie, a few years before, I decided to take a short vacation there, re-acquaint myself with old pals and simply enjoy the sights and sounds of life ashore after three arduous months at sea, prior to continuing on to Montreal to begin preparations for the next field trip. Of course, all too quickly it was time to pack up and leave again, but before departing I made a final visit to the *Theron*. Standing on the dock I admired her smooth lines made for ice navigating; the tall mast with its barrel and the strong re-enforced bows. I had spent a grand time on board her it's true, and would depart with wonderful memories and unforgettable experiences. It was like leaving home.

Back at the *Arctic Unit* in Montreal we sampled and classified some of the Harp seal teeth for age and catalogued other collections of organ specimens in preparation for a later more thorough study. Danny Welch, my cabin mate on the *Theron,* had his film developed and we were entertained with his slide presentation of the voyage. Like the others assembled, I looked forward to viewing the 16 mm film I had made of the seal hunt.. It is difficult to express how enormous the disappointment and how huge the embarrassment was at the time, when we discovered that much of the film was useless due to overexposure. In fact I was horrified. It turned out that the camera on loan from the *National Film Board of Canada* was defective due to a small pin-hole in the apparatus. Of course, there was no way to know this when I made the documentary. Today I feel that an important record of the daily events, showing the exciting and sometimes dangerous lives lived by the sealers, was lost.

The Arctic Unit was at 505 Pine Ave. W. near University St. and the *Royal Victoria Hospital.* I was renting at the time, two rooms on St. Luke St. near Guy and de Maisonneuve,(then Burnside St.), half an hour's walk to work and back each way. On the way home, I often stopped off at the Stork Club on Guy St., a supper club, where customers dined or took a drink at the bar and perhaps danced, if so inclined, to the music of the house band or visiting groups. Latin American Trios like *Los Trios Paragueros*, were all the rage in many bars and clubs in Montreal. Many customers knew their hits and could even sing along to tuneful numbers like *Amour Amour Amour, Besame Mucho*, and *Toda Una Vida* which was known as *Hasta Manana* in the English version, a Bing Crosby hit.

Meanwhile, at *the Arctic Unit*, plans were now well under way for our trip north. Lists of needed equipment were gone over and double-checked: canoes, motors, tents, stoves, gas, oil, fishing nets, boxes, specimen bottles, canned and or dried foods. These were ordered from suppliers to be delivered to the Unit, or to the docks on the river, from where a *Department of Transport* ship would be leaving in early June, on its annual trip north to supply settlements on the arctic islands and around Hudson Bay. We expected to be already in Whale Cove on the scheduled arrival date of the *DOT* vessel to take charge of our gear. There would be plenty of other important cargo unloaded there in addition to ours, vitally required machines and long awaited equipment for the maintenance, well-being, and survival of the community through the long winter ahead. These things could only be brought in during the two months of summer when there was open water in the Bay.

On the way

Finally, the preparations for our trip were completed and we departed from Dorval Airport northward bound, on the first leg of our journey aboard a *Nordair* four-engine North Star. After a brief refuelling stop at Winisk, Ontario on the shores of James Bay, we continued on to Churchill Manitoba, where we intended to spend several days prior to proceeding on to Rankin Inlet. On this, my first visit to Churchill, my time was consumed in contacting government department officials. Most were helpful in providing what we hoped would be useful information for the trip.

There was a small but interesting museum in Churchill, run by the Oblate Fathers. It contained historical mementoes of Church activities in the north and some archaeological and anthropological curiosities: carvings variously in stone and bone, of dolls, sleds, igloos, kayaks, tents and ice-houses. Other human and animal figures depicting various social, play, work (hunting), and religious activities, were presented in different scenic constructions of Inuit life. In reality though, daily life appeared grim for the aboriginal peoples in Churchill in 1962. It was marginally better for the Inuit than for the northern Indians. Maybe this was because the Inuit lived apart in their own campsites while whites - miners, construction workers and others- were forbidden by government policy from fraternizing with them.

We arrived in Rankin Inlet on board an old *C-47 Dakota* aircraft that had obviously seen better flying-days years earlier. It was an interesting experience nevertheless, and it flew remarkably well. Rankin was then, fairly large, keeping in mind this was an Inuit village in the sub-arctic. It consisted of a sort of main street, and a couple of truncated side streets and a dock area on the beach. A dark silhouette, site of the recently abandoned Rankin Nickel Mine, stood sentry in the background. We were given a quick tour of the place a couple of days later. Deep down into the earth, then out under the waters of Hudson Bay we went. The mining authorities had partially flooded the structure in order to secure it, and it was iced up pretty well by then.

We had a few days more of waiting before our boat was ready to leave for Whale Cove. It was a fifty-five foot long-liner, owned and operated by the Whale Cove *FRB* technical projects officer, a jack of all trades and long time resident of the area, who was fluent in *Inuktitut*. I believe he originally came from Manitoba. Usually, one arrived in Whale Cove by air on board a float-plane, so this was turning out to be a more leisurely and enjoyable way of making the journey down the coast, with lots of opportunities to see marine life. The day before sailing was June 21 and the summer solstice, the longest day of the year in the land of the midnight sun. There were almost twenty-four hours of sunlight in Rankin that day. A truly eerie feeling it was. We went out to the local "pub" on one of our last nights in Rankin, where I happened to meet and have a drink with the son of Peter Freuchen, the famous Danish Arctic explorer. He spoke only Inuktitut. Surprisingly, his features were white, although he had the long black hair, brown skin and large lustrous eyes of the Inuit. He was friendly, polite and very tolerant to put up with my questions about his life, responding in a charming and courteous way through the interpreter at our table.

We departed Rankin on a sunny, very calm morning, and set out for Whale Cove. The skipper decided to give us a bit of sight-seeing first, steering north for a look at Chesterfield Inlet the nearest community to Rankin and only a few kilometres away. We passed by famous Marble Island, where we could still clearly see the remains of some of the buildings once a part of the baleen whale processing site. It had been a thriving commercial operation over a century before. Even the small whaler's cemetery, purchased precariously on a rocky outcrop, was still there. A crew member pointed out to me the largest structure in Chesterfield, the Roman Catholic Convent, a landmark for many decades. Afterwards, the skipper swung the long-liner around and we made for Whale Cove, six or seven hours' of sailing time to the south.

To make up time, for we were now running late, the skipper decided to set the vessels mainsail and jib. Away we flew, blown along on a strong following arctic wind and the power of the engines. On the way we made many sightings of ring and harbour seals sitting on rocks along the shore, suning themselves, fishing or playing. I saw my first beluga at this time and became quite excited by the prospects that lay ahead.

About half-way on the trip, a crew member pointed out on the shore a greener spot amidst the sombre tundra lichen. We were asked what we thought could have caused this. No one guessed right. The correct answer, an outhouse, was certainly not apparent: we were many miles from known campsites or settlements and there was no telltale remnant of an earlier construction. There was only that lush patch of green. But it was true. A hundred years before, the Voisey family had migrated to this place from the Labrador shore, following the fish, seals and whales. They probably came just for the summer fishing at first. The temporary visits would become longer until finally, after a few intermarriages with local Inuit, they stayed on. By the 1880's there had been a fine, two-story, frame house constructed there, and other out- buildings as well. There are many Voiseys today in the communities of that region. Indeed, just ahead in Whale Cove, I was to work closely with several members of the Voisey family. The green spot on that shore still marks the family's first permanent homestead away from the Labrador. Nothing else remains. But an occupancy of some fifty or sixty years has left behind this colourful reminder, a nod to the casual passer-by like ourselves that they once had a strong presence there.

At Whale Cove

Its Inuit name *Tikirajuak* means: " *the place where many people arrive"*, or *"meeting place"*, because it was where Inuit assembled to hunt the large numbers of beluga feeding nearby.

Late in the afternoon we arrived in Whale Cove. It would be my home for the next three months. A community of about 80 souls lay within the cove. It was a line of one- room prefab houses strung out along the rim of the crescent-shaped sandy beach. The sides of the cove were rocky and rose gently to meet the lichen-covered tundra that lay just beyond. Whale Cove had been created by the Federal government five or six years earlier, as an experiment. It represented an attempt to get previously nomadic peoples to stay put in one central location so that, various services could be provided efficiently for administrative purposes. The location had been chosen because it was thought to be situated ideally for a people desirous of living off the resources of the land with plenty of arctic char, seals, whales and caribou, available for harvesting. There were actually two diverse groups of people brought together, the nomadic inland *Keewatin* caribou hunters from around Baker Lake, Eskimo Point and points between and the coastal Coral Harbour islander seal hunters. These two groups had lived apart traditionally, meeting only to barter or exchange goods: seal products for caribou products. By now they had lived together for five or six years and I could not tell them apart. Besides, it was summer time, and they were all wearing clothes bought at the Hudson's Bay Store in Rankin Inlet.

To me there seemed to be an enormously large number of dogs in Whale Cove, probably a couple hundred. Actively engaged in hauling sleds over the frozen land and waters of the Bay for most of the year, they now in mid-summer seemed bored and frustrated, tethered to their chains around the clock, full of the bottled up energy of idleness and uselessness. Frequently not fed for long periods, and only watered once daily during the summer months, they were an unruly lot and scary at times, particularly to us *FRB* people. But in truth, let it be known, even their owners only went in amongst them when they were to be fed and watered, and only when armed with a stout heavy stick to maintain order. To try to prevent the dogs from attacking each other, they were tied to a main tethering line as far apart from each other as was practical. They seemed to find this time of year most unpleasant. They were in much better dispositions when the weather turned cold and they were allowed to work and run with the sleds (komatiks). There were large numbers of pups running around freely full of energy and curiosity. They were un-tethered and at liberty to examine and sample any whale carcass remains they came upon - and there were plenty of these left lying around on the rocks after having been flensed of their blubber, and the meat and internal organs removed for human or dog food.

In anticipation of the arrival of the *Department of Transport* vessel, which was due to arrive soon, we were given the possession of a large vacant shed in which we were told we could store the large quantities of gear and food we expected . Another cabin like structure was soon located and taken over by us as a suitable living space. It consisted of a kitchen area, a separate sleeping area fitted out with a half a dozen bunk beds and a storage room. Altogether, not too bad an arrangement for the two of us, so we thought, and we would be staying there only temporarily until our tents came in on the *DOT* vessel. Even during the short time we spent there it turned out to be a busy little "inn", with all bunks constantly occupied by a steady flow of temporary visitors. At times, junior staff members of other research teams or the last arrivals were forced to spend a night or two on the floor in their sleeping bags. During the week that we were guests there and more or less comfortably settled in our bunks, this humble yet popular abode served as home for the high and mighty too. Even some deputy ministers of the crown stayed there. It functioned as an arctic hostel for transient British, French, US and Canadian researchers, mostly anthropologists, but also biologists, economists, and public policy makers. At that time, it seemed that everybody was interested in Whale Cove and what was happening or about to happen there.

Whale Cove was not a pretty place. With the exception of several modern two or three bedroom prefabricated homes set aside for the comfort of the administrator, teacher, senior technical project officer and power generator operator, it consisted of fifty or so single-room prefabricated shacks lying about 250 feet above the high water mark around the cove. All were in a sorry state of disrepair. Scattered around the village were partially full, fifty- gallon oil drums. As well, a couple of twenty-five gallon gasoline drums could be seen near the doorway of each house. Standing somewhat back from the dwellings were even more barrels, now emptied of oil and gas, which served as storage bins for the cut-up beluga whale carcasses or as garbage cans. Many smouldered as their owners tried to burn away some foul smelling material. There was always a strong rancid odour about the place mixed with the smell of whale and seal oil and blubber. Naturally the area was treeless, and the tundra stretched out beyond the village behind some low, uneven, rocky hills and many small ponds. One mercy however, was that the mosquitoes were not too bad compared to the river mouths and estuaries around Rankin Inlet, where they were abundant and ferocious at that time of year. But they were still fierce and numerous and we endured many bloody battles with them. We survived by using a combination of lotions, sprays and protective clothing, covering up completely at sundown. It could have been much worse for us, of course, had we been in Sumatra or Borneo where being bitten could be a matter of life or death. But seeing a cloud of those arctic devils descend on us was enough to send everybody diving for cover.

I thought that for its size Whale Cove needed large quantities of oil brought in to meet daily requirements. A large warehouse dominated the town and was situated squarely in the centre near the beach. A little further off, and slightly smaller stood the power- generating station. The warehouse, although it contained a huge walk-in freezer, served as a meeting hall and social centre, the place where weekly dances were held. All the buildings were erected on props. No digging into the tundra for foundations or basements was permitted: the permafrost lay just below the fragile surface. Even minor damage to the permafrost could set up a rapid process of destructive soil erosion. The cove itself, with its surrounding wide, sandy beach and slopping lichen covered hills was pretty enough but all the man-made parts ruined the natural beauty. I discovered later that almost all arctic communities were eyesores like this one.

Towards the end of my first summer a fierce storm blew down our tent, damaging it so badly that we were forced to abandon it and find refuge in the house of the school teacher. It seemed impressive to us at the time, as we had just spent a couple of months in our ten by eight foot, somewhat dilapidated and decidedly uncomfortable tent. There were two bedrooms, a fully equipped bathroom and kitchen, living room area with broadloom, lamps and stereo system. Not bad for a place like Whale Cove, and the matching salary that went with it was generous, as I soon learned from our host. We only got to stay there for a few days on that first trip north. But on my second visit the following year, after a wall in my tent had been torn open by hungry dogs, I made the short hike from where the tent was set up outside the village, down across the tundra to the teacher's house, whose kind hospitality I graciously accepted, but again only for a few days, as I was just about to leave for home. So it was that on both of my trips to Whale Cove I managed to spend my last few days there in relative luxury.

Within a week of our arrival, the *Dept. of Transport* vessel arrived. She was first spotted away off on the horizon so that by the time she dropped anchor almost two hours later, a large crowd had gathered on the shore. She had come right up to within a hundred yards of the shore outside the cove, anchoring in the deep waters there. Soon there was a flurry of activity everywhere. Large freighter canoes twenty-four feet in length scurried back and forth between the ship and the shore bringing in our cargo and the community's. Pretty soon there were huge mounds of material piled up on the shoreline. It seemed that all the children of the place were there, running helter-skelter, playing games of hide and seek among the large crates and boxes, the coils of rope and the various pieces of heavy equipment. The larger and heavier items had been brought in on board the two Peterhead whalers that were owned by local residents. These very useful boats, around forty feet long, were a commonplace sight in the waters of Hudson Bay for a century, named after their place of origin in Scotland. They were being used now to haul general cargo, and in fishing and hunting. They were powered by a single stroke Grey marine engine and were equipped with sails.

Within a few hours, all of the cargo had been ferried ashore and sat in several large, indistinguishable piles along the beach. We began to rummage through the lot in search of our things, like disembarking airline passengers, in a baggage pickup area, roaming from one revolving carousel to another, without knowing which might hold a sought-for piece of baggage. Eventually we located all of our things and set them aside, so that we soon created our own personal pile, which we then marked. Some little time before, we had discovered the remains of an old, vacated campsite, which had served the needs of some earlier wanderers. Basically, it consisted of a wooden floor, approximately ten by twelve feet, four corner posts and not much more. We decided almost immediately to take it over, and put it to use again. Using a railing that we'd located somewhere serving perfectly as a tent ridge-pole we soon had our tent fitted snugly down around the posts and struts. The site was situated very nicely, sitting just within the protecting cup of a small, rocky ridge. We were no more than 300 feet from the village and less than 600 feet from the shore, where our freighter canoe was moored in a small protected cove. The village water pipe ran along close to our campsite, bringing water from a pond a short distance beyond.

In the big warehouse movie films were shown on Saturday nights and sometimes dances held. I was struck by the popularity of square dance music, Scottish reels and the like, in addition to the ever- present country music. On occasion, I was fortunate enough to witness a spontaneous concert of ancient Inuit dance and drum music and song performed mainly by elders. But mostly, it was the fiddle or accordion music which, perhaps not surprisingly, captured the people's imagination and emotions and bade them join in a jig, a reel or a waltz. Although they seemed shy, modest people, they certainly wasted no time in getting out on the dance floor of a Saturday night to show off their stuff, which was a strange mixture of Celtic step-dance moves and Inuit drum dance "stomp". It was at such times as these that I was glad I remembered to bring my guitar, and thankful to the generous people of the village for letting me share these special occasions. One happy gathering of Inuit and 'visitor- kablunas ' from the south, including some bureaucrats and political types took place out on the tundra one fine summer evening almost by chance. With a generous supply of mass wine someone managed to obtain from the local French *Oblate* father, a good meal of bannock and caribou steaks tasted just that much better and we didn't seem to mind the gnats and bugs at all on that occasion.

During that first summer in Whale Cove our local Inuit helper was a man named Sugi or Suki. He had been recommended to us because he was said to be very good with nets and around canoes and boats. This was really not a very good arrangement in some ways, because he knew no English and we knew very little Inuktitut. This often led to misunderstandings and badly bungled work assignments. Of course, all three of us were guilty in this respect. Whenever this happened, which was often, we would take a cigarette break and try to resolve the immediate problem. Now, David was only a social smoker, and I was a smoker trying to quit, so these breaks pleased nobody but Suki. He was thoroughly addicted and seemed to love every minute of this addiction. In fact, he was never seem without his cigarette. Suki, short and stocky but with good body strength was never to be seen without a cigarette. It was always stuck securely in his mouth and he never seemed to have to handle it. Always working with his hands, which were wet or dirty from handling nets, arctic char, grayling, beluga and seals, he had learned how to enjoy a good smoke without wasting good tobacco. I will always remember Suki, and the great smile he had for me, no matter how grey the day. I can picture him standing there in the canoe, less than five feet tall, enveloped in a fog of cigarette smoke.

Catching Beluga

Within a few days we had put out our first sixteen inch mesh net. Shortly after, we had our first beluga. By this time, a number of nets had been set out by the men of the village, although it was still early in the summer and the sea ice had only just left. A number of beluga had already been caught, cut up and stored in barrels around the village. Now, it was my turn, to first observe and then learn, under the careful guidance of Suki, the art and the science of flensing a whale. Only a long, sharp knife was required, to get the job done quickly and easily. A single circular stroke around the neck, then a long straight incision made from the neck cut straight down along the length of the belly to another circular cut near the tail. Two longitudinal incisions, along the length of the animal on its dorsal surface, completed the major essential cuts needed to flense the beluga. Afterwards, the flensor made smaller incisions, which usually cut out twenty by forty inch sections, that connected the longtitudional cuts. These sections contained the outer skin or *muktuk,* and the underlying layer of blubber which was usually three to five inches thick. When the blubber was removed, the underlying skeleton containing the meat was easily cut up into sections and stored in barrels. This would serve as dog food for the months ahead, until the ice returned in the fall. The soft, internal organs and some of the better cuts of meat were for the people to be eaten fresh or, frozen, and eaten later. *Muktuk* was regarded as a tasty snack for nibbling on by anybody who came around during the flensing process. I often nibbled on *muktuk* myself, and liked its nutty flavour. The entire operation of flensing and butchering took about half an hour for an eighteen foot animal. Most of the animals we took samples from that summer were caught in these large mesh nets, but some were still killed in the traditional old way of harpooning or shooting: the animals would become entangled in the mesh and, unable to surface to breath, drowned.

By mid July there were twenty or twenty-five nets set, half of them by David, Suki and me, which were checked daily. Before summer's end a total of 180 beluga whales were caught and processed for food. David and I extracted the canine teeth, and collected stomach contents and reproductive organs from these animals, in order to use them in population studies later in the lab. The rings on the canine teeth, similar to those on the trunks of trees, were counted from microscopic sections and used to estimate the animals' ages. Occasionally, pregnant females were caught in the nets and their perfectly formed baby foetuses, pinkish blue in colour and about six to eight inches long, were removed from the uterus and preserved in alcohol, to be examined later in the lab. Only one calf is generally born every two years, so the species does not replace itself rapidly. The baby when born is dark blue or even brown in colour, then, as it matures the colour changes and it passes through lighter and lighter shades of blue until it reaches the greyish colour of adolescence, which finally evolves into the bright white of the adult. This process takes more than 10 years to complete. Animals that were still alive in Inuit nets when they went to inspect them, were killed by shots from a high-powered rifle, a .220 or, a .222. Sometimes highly prized ring or harbour seals were taken in the nets along with whales. The women of the village separated the valuable seal skins from the carcasses and prepared them for making clothes.

Although hunting beluga by harpoon and guns was not commonly seen, I was awakened one Sunday morning to the noise of rifle fire, which along with the hooting and shouting of many hunters signalled a good old - fashioned whale drive. Rushing to the cove, I was just in time to catch the tail end of this activity. A herd of about thirty belugas had been cornered by fifteen or twenty men hunting from their canoes, forcing them into the shallow reaches of the cove where they were shot and harpooned. In the two summers I spent in Whale Cove, this was the only time I witnessed a pod of whales of this size come close enough to the village to be trapped.

The nets for catching beluga were sixteen inch mesh, 100 to 130 feet in length, and fifteen feet deep. They were sometimes anchored to the shore by tying them to large rocks, and at other times, anchored to the bottom in shallow estuaries and inlets. They were never set in deep water and one could usually see the bottom from the surface. Dead and dying whales attract a number of other sea-life forms, and these creatures could be seen feeding on the whales' skin. Among these sea-life forms were spider and hermit crabs and a variety of spiders. The appearance of sea lice was a common one, both on living and dead beluga. As the animals were being hauled to the surface to the canoe the spiders and crabs could be seen scurrying off the skin and diving back into the cold waters of Hudson Bay. The lice however generally stayed put.

Seldom was more than one animal caught in a net at any one time, but occasionally there were two or more. All died from drowning, caught in the nets at different depths below the surface but usually towards the bottom. Occasionally a whale was discovered to be still alive because it was caught near the net's top and could surface for air. I will always carry with me one unforgettable encounter during my second summer in Whale Cove. Solomon, my assistant and interpreter that year, and I, came upon what seemed to be an entire family of beluga caught in a net. Two of the animals both young adults, were already drowned near the bottom of the net. Two other adults near the top of the net, continued to surface and blow. Most amazing, was the presence of a baby calf, less than a week old.

The beluga calf was very frightened, confused and in a state of obvious distress, for it kept darting about from the living to the dead members of the pod. It surfaced next to the canoe several times, resting momentarily on the surface, easily allowing us to reach out and gently stroke it along its body and snout. Then, it dove down to where the dead animals were, circling them, before returning to the side of the canoe. It appeared to us, that one of the dead whales was probably the calf's mother. We felt helpless and hypnotized with sadness for the living animals, especially the pitiful calf.

What we eventually decided on and perhaps the only practical thing to do was to return as quickly as possible to our camp. We retrieved the camera in order to record the sight and the rifle in order to put the survivors out of their misery. The round trip took us half an hour. As we approached the net on our return, we found everything quiet, no animal surfacing to blow as we expected. The two adult beluga, alive earlier, were now also drowned. Way down at the bottom of the net, near the dead animal that we assumed was the mother, we saw the small, dark form of the calf, entangled in the net and now dead, too.

Looking back on it, I wondered if we did the right thing. We could have released the two living animals from the net, and perhaps one of the two might be able to nurse the calf. But then again, that probably would not have occurred.

Many years later, I had a similar experience. It was in Costa Rica during the rainy season. Several of us were travelling along a river by launch when we came across a herd of cattle marooned on a sliver of dry land with the water rising around it and hungry crocodiles all about. In the midst of this stormy scene, we saw a calf fall off the bank into the turbulent water. The calf pawed helplessly at the muddy bank, bleating for its mother standing just above. While the rest of us thought the calf's predicament helpless, our guide, Willis Rankin, brought the launch close to the bank. He left the tiller, came forward, and from the bow reached down and grasped the calf by its ears. He pulled it on board, held it securely for a moment, then heaved it onto the land; it ran to its mother. We gave Willis a great round of applause, to which he modestly replied that he had lots of practice doing that sort of thing. In all my travels on several continents, Willis was one of the nicest, most admirable people I have ever met. I was reminded again that day in Costa Rica of the tragic sight of the baby whale and I think of it often.

I take up hunting.

When I first went north, I was unaware of the great importance placed on hunting in Inuit social and cultural life. Although I had been issued with a rifle along with all my other stores by the Fisheries Research Board, I hadn't yet used it, even though I had been there a couple of weeks. By contrast, the Inuit hunters had their guns with them at all times. When they were not actually hunting, they busied themselves in target practice. I began to suspect that they thought this behaviour a bit odd. I mentioned this to Solomon and he confirmed my suspicions. He told me I would be held in higher regard if I managed to bag an animal and, in fact, they were waiting to see if I could.

After my talk with Solomon, I kept the gun in the canoe with me during our trips to the nets. I waited for a hunting opportunity to come along, and sure enough, one sunny, dead calm morning, I spotted our quarry. It was a ring seal, not more than a hundred feet from the boat. It alternately surfaced for a short time, its head bobbing, and disappeared into long dives. During one of these rests at the surface, I got off two or three shots from the .222. We sped over to the kill, in order to retrieve it before it had time to sink. Several people were on the beach later that evening, when we arrived, to bear witness to our success. Not only this, but Solomon spread the word among his friends. My personal stock noticeably improved: I was now valued as a hunter as well as accepted as a friend. I must confess, though, that on the night I killed the seal I felt I was visited by its spirit.

Dogs were still the main mode of getting around in 1962. Whale Cove had seventy to eighty people, one snowmobile, and more than 200 dogs. At night, there was frequently a great racket of dog-song. Usually one dog would begin howling and others would join in so that it sounded like all the dogs in Whale Cove were howling in unison. Sometimes there were showdowns between individuals or groups. Strangely, these concerts often died out within minutes but at other times they dragged on interminably for hours.

In 1960 or '61, I had noticed in some of the higher priced shops in Montreal and Toronto new, made -in- Canada foods, arctic meats like seal and whale, and arctic fishes such as arctic char and grayling. I had tried some and had liked some. At the time, I knew nothing about their origins or histories. It was only when I started working at the *FRB* that I first heard about Otto and his arctic canning enterprise. He hoped to develop this into a resource- based industry, a source of employment for aboriginal peoples throughout the area. The Federal Government was trying out these products in select Canadian markets, to see if they might catch on. They hoped eventually to expand into choice markets like New York and European capitals, marketing these products as exotic gourmet *"in"* foods for the 1960's. But things were still in the experimental stage in 1962, when I first met Otto in Whale Cove.

The operation consisted of only a couple of small shacks near the beach, and in addition to Otto, only one or two other Inuit workers. Nobody had any clear idea about the possible outcome of the venture, although somebody in Government had seen that enough financial resources were channelled into the undertaking to operate a small cannery. Otto ran the operations side of the venture, but I'm sure he had some input into the marketing side of things also, for he was a man of great enthusiasm and energy and had strong opinions on everything. There he was, this recently arrived immigrant from Germany, rushing around in his rubber apron, supervising the preparation of fish and meats for canning. He had large steam vats or cooking boilers containing arctic char, seal meat, and sometimes beluga. Also on the site were machines for packing and covering the cans. The operation seemed to run smoothly several days a week, but there were many down days too, due mainly to difficulties in acquiring or replacing parts in this remote and isolated setting.

I remember above all the unpleasant odours of the canning process, odours that kept unwanted visitors at a distance. Perhaps Otto wanted it this way, to ensure privacy. In addition to the sheds there was a washing and cleaning area, and the whole site was enclosed behind a low fence of plastic, possibly to hide the goings- on from the inquisitive stares of the children. Later that year, I happened to see some of Otto's products at a trendy food shop in Toronto's Colonade on Bloor St. and felt a glow of pride remembering their humble origins. So, I thought, at least he can boast of having got his cans this far.

The ice was out of the Bay, and we could work there from our freighter canoes and Peterhead whalers without its hindrance by the end of June. Also, the weather had become reasonably mild and even comfortable, and would remain so until September, when early winter conditions would return to this part of *Keewatin.* The prevailing winds along the north-west coast of Hudson Bay are northeasters, and they bring cold rains. Luckily, stormy weather forced us to get up during the night, to tighten tent guy ropes, or secure tent pegs, only a few times during our first summer there. Indeed, there were many pleasant or even warm days, with temperatures climbing up to 20 or more degrees Centigrade, although generally it was about 15-18 degrees.

The waters of the Bay were always cold, which made it always uncomfortable work, struggling to untangle beluga and seals from the nets, before towing them ashore. Sometimes they were so badly tangled in the nets, that it was necessary to cut away that part of the animal most heavily entangled, usually a fluke or tail, in order to free the animal for transport. Our net catches included animals of both sexes, and from all age groupings, so that we had samples of all sizes and colours of animals- greys, browns, blues, and the bright whites of mature adults. Once we found in a net, a deformed adult beluga, with a strange hump on its back. No one seemed to know the cause of this arcane curiosity, for it seemed to be in an otherwise excellent state of health. Hypotheses to explain this mystery ranged from obvious probable causes to wildly unlikely ones. The more reasonable guesses included genetic birth defects, and injuries from polar bear or killer whale attack. Whatever the cause, it remained a magnet for curious visitors, and a popular subject of photographs before it too, was flensed and cut up like the others.

Inuit children were always a delight and joy. While at play, they constantly radiated their enthusiasm and happiness at being alive, and the freedom they felt at exploring their surroundings. Mischievous and curious, they made what otherwise might be boredom for others, pass quickly by inventing clever ways to amuse and stimulate themselves. There were only twenty-five or thirty little ones under ten in Whale Cove, and only a few older children of school age, since most of the inhabitants were young married couples. Only a few middle-aged or older Inuit lived in the settlement as it had been created only five years before. Older Inuit would not have wanted to leave their previous homes in much longer settled villages.

The school teacher, from Nova Scotia, a man of perhaps 40, had already spent ten or fifteen years teaching in the Arctic, at the time I was there. He had managed to put away a sizeable nest-egg, almost enough to return home permanently, and live in splendid early retirement. There was also a French Catholic priest, an Oblate, who too had lived ten or fifteen years in the Arctic. Another *kabluna* (white person) residing permanently in the settlement was a fundamentalist Protestant preacher from the *US* who, along with his family, had made this his new ministry. He too was a long term resident of the north, and was well set up to manage his ministry affairs there. He had shown inventive talent in the construction of his working sailboat, made from materials found around the place. He out-fitted one of the ubiquitous 24 foot freighter canoes with a mast, rudder and sails. There was in 1962 no ordained Anglican priest in Whale Cove, but only a lay person, to attend to that church's interests. But that really wasn't a disadvantage that I could see, for a person wasn't aligned to any one church congregation, not in a permanent sense at any rate. They moved freely from one church group to another, as they felt inclined, without showing the least sign of embarrassment or social discomfort. Maybe a ceremonious catholic mass to start the day would seem suitable on Sundays, followed by an enlivening, fundamentalist gospel hour in the afternoon; finally the evensong service at the Anglican hall, for winding down and ending the day. It seemed perfectly reasonable to everyone, as long as one had the time to squeeze in all three attendances. By following this regimen, no one would feel upset or slighted by neglect.

There lived in the Cove a crippled man, of about 65. He lived alone and seemed to spend all of his time lying upon a large, untidy, and dirty bed placed towards the back of his one roomed shack. But he had many visitors and was seldom alone. One was left to wonder why this was so, for, in addition to the many friends and close relatives who attended to his daily needs, there were always plenty of others milling around, by day and night. He never left, perhaps could not, leave the shack and I saw him only once not on the bed. That one time, looking from the entrance doorway, I saw him moving around with difficulty on crutches inside the room. The mystery surrounding him was explained to me in time by the preacher. I was told that the shut-in ran a gambling den in the form of nightly card games. Almost anything of value was being used to gain entrance to the games. The stakes were high- and even included gambler's wives who thus became the shut-in's unwilling sexual partners. Eventually, these unhappy and very angry ladies told the clergy. The priest and preacher in turn relayed the wives' accounts to the area administrator. Acting together, the administrator, the priest, and the preacher, managed to bring to an end this tawdry affair. I believe all that was needed to do this was a friendly visit to the shut-in and a bit of friendly persuasion.

One day some hunters returning from a trek inland, informed us that a huge caribou herd was quite near the village, moving north on their annual migration. This caused great excitement among the people, and a number of hunting parties were soon mounted and left to intercept the herd. Within a few days the first party returned with a supply of fresh meat and everybody in the cove was soon settling down to enjoy savoury tundra steaks for a week

These were in the days when the people of Whale Cove attempted still to live off the land- the Government's stated reason for moving there in the first place. Already, even then, there seemed to be too much dependence on Hudson Bay stores and they were becoming a people in limbo. They were neither northerners like their parents nor southerners like the people they were seeing on the television sets newly arriving, or in the movies. The old values were coming under attack and crumbling.

There were always a number of semi-wild dogs running around freely on the surrounding tundra. These dogs would often make scavenging raids into the village, in search of food left unattended or to get at the whale meat stored in the recycled oil drums. One day, I foolishly left an open can of beef in the tent, before leaving on my rounds of the nets. Now, ordinarily this food would have been locked up in a metal box, and stored outside the tent somewhere, or even buried in the earth above the permafrost. Upon my return, I was confronted by a tent without an intact wall. The hunger of the dogs had been so intense, that it overcame their fear of people.

Once, during the visit of a couple of French scientists, I accompanied them for a walk out over the tundra as it was a fine summer's evening. From a small rocky outcropping we heard dogs howling, and upon investigating, discovered that one of them had been unable to run off because its tethering chain had become wedged in the crevasse of a rock. One of the Frenchmen approached the dog and quickly freed it. Indeed, the dog showed more fear than he. The dog had probably not been trapped very long, for it appeared strong and alert, and the other dogs still accompanying it.

I cannot say that I had any part in the rescue-I had stood back, watching apprehensively, along with the other Frenchman – nor can I be sure that the bold action in freeing the dog saved its life. Probably the owner would soon have missed it and gone looking.

However well intentioned the government policies, there were soon serious misunderstandings and mistakes being made by officials on the ground and at various levels of bureaucracy. We now know how wrong-headed and wasteful these policies often were. *The Royal Commission Report* of June 1994 on Inuit relocation shows this clearly and powerfully. It details the *Department of*

Northern and Indian Affairs' coerced move of individual Inuit and family groups from Port Harrison, Quebec, and "recruits" from Pond Inlet, *District of Keewatin,* to Resolute Bay and Grise Fjord in the high arctic in 1955. The Government under pressure offered repatriation in 1988, which resulted in splitting families along generational lines and the population plummeting. Inuit organizations claim that the forced exiles of 1955 were the unwitting pawns of Government in a bid to reinforce its claim to Devon and Ellesmere Islands.

Farley Mowat, author of the still popular, moving and informative memoir *'People of the Deer'*, published in 1952, dealt in part with the many bewildering and harmful Government policies of the day. I remember him being held up as an object of ridicule by several people from the *Department of Northern and Indian Affairs* in 1962, but during my time living and working in the north I increasingly began to feel that he was spot-on in his biting criticisms of Government policy.

I had a friend in Whale Cove named Kalugjuak. He was a black Eskimo, in the same sense that Freuchen's son was a white Eskimo. I was surprised the first time I saw him and his younger brother who was also black, although in hindsight I should not have been. They were returning to the Cove from a hunting trip on board their Peterhead whaler. It was a pretty smart looking boat of about forty-five feet, equipped for hunting and fishing as well as hauling freight along the coast. With Solomon acting as interpreter, I was able to converse with the brothers and to hire their services for my summer work.

Kalugjuak, I learned, was 40 years old and the father of five children. His brother was much younger, perhaps 25. They believed their black ancestor was a cook on a New England commercial whaler in the nineteenth century who, foreseeing a better life for himself in the Arctic, had jumped ship there. Like Freuchen's son they were completely assimilated into Inuit culture.

In 1962, the proscription against fraternizing between miners, construction workers, and other whites on one hand and Inuit on the other was in full force. It was already well known by then, the ravishes of alcohol abuse and mindless sexual promiscuity that it so often lead to had undermined and utterly destroyed the cultural values of aboriginal peoples to the south. The non-fraternization rule was meant to spare the Inuit the same fate. We now know that there were other evil abuses perpetrated on the helpless peoples of the north, chief among them the residential schools.

There were neither handicrafts nor soapstone carvings in Whale Cove, as in Rankin Inlet and Churchill, where there were several artists and artisans of exceptional ability. In time, they acquired international reputations as soapstone carvers, their work commissioned and sold under Government supervision to collectors in the south and abroad. The business of commissioning and marketing soapstone carvings and other Inuit art was a new one at that time, perhaps only a decade old. This was due almost single-handedly to its exposure to an increasingly interested world by James Houston, the internationally renowned Canadian teacher, artist and writer, when he was living and working out of Cape Dorset, Baffin Island. The only carver I knew who sold his work privately under his own name as well as under his Government issued ID number was Mamatsiak, E5-123. I last saw him in the TB sanatorium in Churchill where he was being treated while recovering from tuberculosis. I also have a couple of souvenir pieces only known to me as - E 91032 and E 91211 who were fellow artist carvers in the Churchill San along with Mamatsiak. During a ramble once, I picked up from the land wash of a nearby beach to the

Cove an odd rough little carved bear six inches long, a similar example of which I saw years later in the McCord Museum in Montreal.

Practically all the women of Whale Cove were capable seamstresses and sewers, and all could be persuaded to show off their interestingly embroidered parka and mukluk creations many with intricate crossed-stitch designs. I had several pairs of attractive mukluks made which I later gave to appreciative friends in the south.

Beverly Borens, a well-known Toronto Inuit art dealer and collector and until recently a frequent visitor into Canada's arctic communities attended one of my slide show talks and informed me afterwards that things were still very much the same in Whale Cove, as when I was working there. It has remained a resource based activities settlement where people can be seen wearing traditional skin clothing, employing dog sleds, *(Komatiks)*, in winter, and eating raw fish and meat (*maktor).* If true, Whale Cove would seem to have remained as traditional a community as isolated Grise Fjord, Canada's most northerly settled community on Ellesmere Island .

I spent my second summer, that of 1963, in Whale Cove alone. I made the trip to Churchill from Montreal with *Nordair* Airlines as before, with a fuelling stopover in Winisk on James Bay, Ontario. It was a four- engine prop plane, with seats for only about 20 passengers placed along one side of the plane with the freight and baggage stacked along the opposite bulkhead. Before proceeding on to Whale Cove I had been asked to make an aerial survey of the beluga whale population in the waters of Hudson Bay, around Churchill. Being early summer, the beluga pod sizes were still quite large during this their mating season and many females had already calved.

To help me conduct the survey, I had been given the name of a bush pilot in Churchill, whose services I chartered to fly me over the Bay waters around Churchill. After contacting him we arranged a meeting. My aerial survey consisted of counting all the animals I could see, using a hand held clicker to keep score, as the total numbers were not expected to be very great. Our plane was the workhorse of the Arctic, the Beaver, a small two-seater float-plane, with storage space for only a couple of small bags behind the two seats up front. For hauling heavier loads of freight or more passengers, the larger Norseman or the even larger still Otter were used. After a brief "chummy" discussion about the work I needed done, we set out the following morning. I climbed into the passenger seat and with Bob at the controls we took off. It was my first water take-off in a float plane and a first time for me to be sitting up front with the pilot, as my earlier trips into Whale Cove the previous summer had been made by boat from Rankin Inlet.

We decided to make daily flights out over the Bay around Churchill, everywhere there were whales to be seen and I would attempt to count as many as possible. The animals were expected to number in total only several hundred at this time of year. This counting method with the clicker certainly was not as complicated as those we'd used for estimating the seal populations in our aerial surveys off Labrador several years before. There, huge numbers were involved, perhaps hundreds of thousands, and total herd counts had to be estimated from photographs taken of cross-sections of the herd. Final counts would then be done back in the lab from the photographs, and extrapolations made for final total counts. After several days of flying I reckoned that I had enough material. I had taken several dozen photos of the beluga pods as well as doing the counts, chiefly in order to see how well I could judge the pod composition with regard to sex, age and family composition. To get these, the pilot would dive down from several hundred feet and sweep across the surface of the water, to within twenty or twenty-five feet of the surface, where I would take my pictures. Luckily for me, by concentrating on the belugas just below, sometimes only a few feet away, I managed to keep my anxiety levels at a minimum. Bob was a first rate flyer though and not one to be tempted by showing off with attempting dangerous stunts, in order for me to get the pictures I wanted. Usually, groups of five or six whales were seen, although occasionally larger ones of 20 or more were also turning up. On rare occasions, solitary males could be seen approaching from further up the Bay. On our way back to base following these daily counting runs, Bob let me take the controls and "fly" the plane for a while, which was quite a thrill.

During my two summers working in the arctic, I had taken flights in both the Norseman and Otter as well as the Beaver. Often, the Norseman was the frequent flyer into Whale Cove, usually bringing in the mail and a passenger or two, on its weekly service. At times, the water in the cove was so rough that the pilot would be forced to make several attempts at a take-off before finally striking enough calm water to get airborne. There were occasions when we spent the better part of an hour attempting but failing to get into the air. At the time there were rumours going around about the unreliability of the Norseman under conditions such as these. I never experienced any problems however using this aircraft, although it had been involved in some scary fatal crashes from time to time. The Otter was being used more like a mini bus. It was the largest of the three float planes and could seat as many as ten passengers with storage space for their baggage.

My interpreter and assistant during my second summer in the Cove was Solomon, a lad of fifteen, who lived with his mother Annie, then about forty-five. She was a descendant of the Voiseys who had come over to Kewatin from Labrador in the 1880's. Like all the Voiseys she was dark skinned with

Caucasian features. Solomon had a brother Lewis of about twenty-five, also living in Whale Cove. He was married to a pretty young Inuit girl, also named Annie, about eighteen years of age. Lewis was soft- spoken and fluent in both Inuktitut and English, more white in appearance than either Solomon or their mother Annie and had been brought up as white. You would have mistaken him for someone from the south if you didn't know better. Only recently married, Lewis and Annie still childless, had the energy and time to be actively involved in many community activities. He was the opposite to his indifferent and lackadaisical half brother Solomon, who was more of an annoyance than a help to me at times. He seemed to have had a different kind of upbringing than Lewis, perhaps one without the presence of a suitable role model to act as a guide for him. However, there was something endearingly amusing about Solomon, something which he affected without effort, and it was that "something" which bonded us during our summer working together.

I remember getting mad with Solomon only twice. The first time was when he almost drowned the two of us. While trying unsuccessfully to get the outboard Johnson motor started one day, in his frustration he forgot to check on the position of the rudder. When finally the engine "*kicked in*" under an almost wide open throttle, the canoe began racing around the Cove wildly, tracing out wide arcs and narrowly missing other canoes and rocky reefs. The second occurred after he'd been failing repeatedly to arrive for work at our previously agreed upon start-up times. It was this bad habit of his that lead me to finally go over to his mother's house, and haul him out of bed. Annie his mother, who also happened to be my laundress and baker, had lectured him about this laziness of his many times but to no avail. But because of her valuable services to me up to that point I was of course anxious to maintain our good relations , and refrained from "blowing my stack" because of Solomon's truancy. I remember all of the

Voiseys with great warmth and affection to this day, for they made my stay in the Cove a comfortable and enjoyable one.

Although several thousand kilometres from home, I nevertheless discovered that it was still a very small world indeed, for one day a long-liner sailed into the Cove from Rankin, Captained by Ches Russell who just by chance, happened to be the uncle of my father's housekeeper back in St. John's, Newfoundland. It was a totally unexpected and serendipitous first meeting for us both, and after we realised the uniqueness of this connection, we spent a long while afterwards chatting about our many other common interests of home. Russ worked for the Federal Government, and travelled about, to wherever he was needed. He commanded many useful talents and was known throughout the North as a "fixer-upper", particularly in those places where new ventures were being started up. He was then fifty-five, a large, solid, outgoing, and fun loving fellow from Bay Roberts, a typical Conception Bay, Newfoundland man. Like the preacher, the French priest, the Voiseys, the technical projects person and even our area administrator, he was a man who had spent over twenty years living in the arctic. All these individuals considered themselves to be permanent residents of the North, and all spoke fluent Inuktitut. I too soon realized that to be truly engaged in any meaningful way with my Inuit workmates it would be necessary for me to learn some Inuktitut. So within days of my arrival, I started putting together my own personal dictionary of many practical Inuktitut words and expressions.

Between my first and second years in Whale Cove there had been two fundamental changes in my life, which resulted in changing my plans with *FRB*. I had returned to Dalhousie University to complete my undergraduate studies and begin graduate work in Marine Biology, and while there I had got married. But this returning to the university by me had resulted in David Sergeant, my

FRB supervisor, having to go out on the seal hunt again in my place, and I knew that he had grown very weary of this specific field project. It could be a particularly unpleasant and even dangerous job at times, and he had a wife and young family to consider. The one trip that I had made *"to the ice"* was enough for me, and I was happy to avoid having to do that again. I did however agree to return to Whale Cove for a second summer, and this time alone, so that he would be relieved of having to spend that summer also away from his family.

By the second week in September the ground was beginning to harden overnight with early autumn frost, and already the first snowflakes had begun to fall. The ice flows could be seen approaching from the north, and soon the Bay would be covered by them. The beluga would then become inaccessible to us by netting. As in the previous year, it was now time to pack up and leave the Cove. I got a ride out to the waiting Otter in a freighter canoe for a last time, for I knew that I probably would not be returning this way again. It was a beautiful clear, crisp, autumn morning, the waters were almost calm and the surrounding tundra and village seemed to be dozing in the early morning light. It was as if I were observing them in a painting. I was about to get out of the canoe when something sort of spooky happened, for just as I was about to climb from the canoe to the float of the plane, the leather strap on my rather special and expensive wristwatch unhitched and fell into the Cove's waters. It felt as if I was leaving behind a token of some kind to this loveable, if somewhat scruffy, little place. We took off uneventfully however and reached Rankin Inlet within an hour.

At that time, the flights from Rankin to Churchill were made in old, World War Two surplus twin-engine Dakotas, which were operated by either *Nordair*, or *Transair*. There were seats for only a dozen or so passengers, with the remaining space reserved for cargo. It was a chilly and noisy ride inside these aircraft down to Churchill from Rankin that normally took a couple of hours. From there, a four engine *North Star* made the flight back to Montreal, via Winisk. Now and then, the return flights were routed back to Montreal through Winnipeg, the headquarters for *Nordair.*

Working for the *FRB* had provided me with some great employment experience, and plenty of valuable information about the marine mammal world of whales and seals, internationally as well as nationally. So it was with excitement that I learned shortly after my return to Montreal and later Dalhousie in Halifax, of a number of attractive job offers. I thought three of them in particular were interesting enough to track down. The first was the offer of a position aboard a Japanese whale hunting ship in the Pacific, logging the longitudinal and latitudinal positions of whale sightings, and catches. A second similar offer was that aboard a Norwegian whale hunter making similar recordings of whale sightings and kills in the Atlantic. Both of these positions had opened up because of an increased interest being shown by the *International Whaling Commission.* The third interesting offer was quite different from the other two and involved a combination of academic, research and field work. The offer was from the *Cetacean Research Laboratory,* in Torrance, California. It was a privately funded organisation with UCLA connections. Although I haven't heard anything about it in decades and it may no longer exist, it seemed an interesting place at the time. It really didn't matter anyway. As it turned out, none of these offers did. I had decided to turn my back on the seas with some regret, and to walk away in search of other kinds of adventures.

Part Four : To the Present

Tin Whistles Blowin' That Nobody Hears

Come gather around and a short tale I'll tell,
About a once proud sailin' queen,
And the strange man who sailed her on a November swell,
And sunk her in ship's hole unseen.

A hard wind was throwing down hail all around,
The headland's still covered by the oceans big sound,
So come all ye children if ya listen you'll hear,
A tin whistle's blowin' that nobody hears.

Now the weather was right as they sailed out of sight,
And the sound of the riggin' was fine ,
But away down the shoreline somewhere in the night,
They were breathin' down water by nine.

And the boswain's tin whistle played over that moat,
And still he kept playin' not missing a note.
So come all ye children if ya listen you'll hear,
A tin whistle's blowin' that nobody hears.

Now this story I tell you, as it was told to me,
How you'll hear that pipe playing today,
Some night in November when the ocean's crazy,
Hear that boswain keep playing away.

So try to remember when you go out tonight,
About that old boswain, John Samuel Wright,
And come all of ye children if ya listen you'll hear,
A tin whistle's blowin' that nobody hears.

84

A)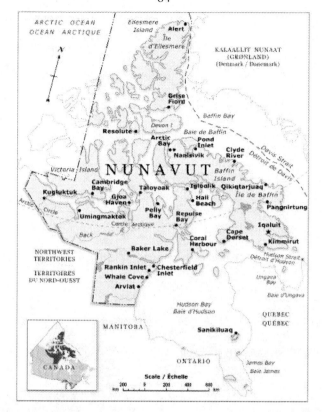

B)

A)

B)

C)

A)

B)

C)

A Newfoundland Toast

Rum, Oh! Rum, you are my pest,

You often made me lose my rest,

You often made me wear bad clothes,

You often made my friends my foes,

But since you are so near my nose,

Let's tip it off and down she goes,   (Anon)

Sammy Morgan Revisited

A stranger tale I could never tell about the place wherein I dwell,

There are no lights the walls are strong, upon the floor I lay so long,

From there I heard an awful sound, I rose I stumbled from a hound,

A host of creatures all appeared, mostly dark and mostly weird.

There're mice so large they're out of sight ,

 Standing by my door tonight ,

A great big rooster blocked the way, collecting tickets,

 I must say it really was a sight to see,

A donkey even talked to me.

A team of monkies in my hall, began to play a game of ball.

 I somehow made my bed upstairs,

 I fell onto it full of fears,

 I still could hear the rooster call,

 My ceiling then began to fall.

 I woke today a' well past noon and all seemed normal in my room,

 I looked within the mirror there, my old familiar self was there.

A Short Glossary of Newfoundland words , from

The Dictionary of Newfoundland English, and friends or family.

Arn = any

Bawl = a crying

Bedlamer = a one year old seal, also a youth 12-16 years of age

Beer = used by St. John's children as refered to soft drinks

Brewis = a meal of boiled or fried hardtack and pork scrunchings

Chucklehead = a stupid person

Chinch = to stow tightly

Chokey = prison (from British India)

Cotillian = quadrille like dance

Cracked = crazy

Doter = an old seal

Drung = a narrow rocky lane

Duff = a pudding of flour, fat pork and molasses

Faggot = a pile of half dried fish

The 'fat' = the harp seal herds

Flippers = the seal's shoulder, arm and paw, a delicacy in

Newfoundland, usually baked as a pie.

Frankgum= resin from fir evergreen used as chewing gum

Gaff = long pole ending in a heavy hook, with several uses

Gob = mouth

Hardtack = hard bread, as used in fish and brewis

Harp = A Harp seal

Heft = to weigh in the hand

Hood (old dog) = a large (eight ft.) male hood seal

Huffed = vexed. Huff = angry

Hummock = a small hill

The"ice" = the ice floes where the seals are having their young

(A ' berth to the ice' = a sleeping space available on sealing ship)

Jannies (Janneying) = masquerading time practiced in the outports during the 12 days of Christmas, also known as mummering (mummers), featuring house to house visiting with accompanied singing, dancing and usually strong drink.

Jinker = one who brings bad luck

Lancers = a quadrille like dance, with 4 pairs and 5 figures(sets)

Logy = groggy, as with a hangover

Longers = long rails for a fence

Lops = small breaking seas. Loppy = small rough seas

Mauzy = misty, sultry

Mug-up = The Nfld. coffee break, with tea replacing coffee

Narn = none

Nish = tender

The "patches" =   the whelping seals on the ice floes

Raggedy-Jacket = a seal's patchy coat, following the shedding

of the white coat, about a month after birth.

Rawny = boney, very thin

Scrawb = to tear with the nails

Slob = newly frozen ice

Smidge= a stain

Sliveen = a deceitful or rougish person

Splits = small pieces of cut up kindling to keep the fire going

Shavings = wood shavings to help start the fire

Squish = sound of water exuding from boots

Swig = to drink from bottle

Swiller =   a seal hunter

Switchel = cold tea

A 'time' = a party or dance

Traipse = to walk around unnecessarily or aimlessly

Tuckamore = a low clump of trees

Yaffle = an armful of dried fish

Yer = 'here', some Newfoundlanders drop their h's or put them

when they shouldn't.

Yap = to retort angrily

A Few Newfoundland Sayings

Mind yer mouth now = admonishing someone that their language is a off colour.

Any mummers 'loud in ? = asked by a dressed up mummer when the ower of the house answers the door

Beatin' da pat = walking or hanging around the roads.

Me 'ead feels right logy after the time last nite = someone suffering a hangover

Now luh, da arse is gone right out of 'er = the economy has totally collapsed

"Don't pick the red ones they're green" = told to a child not to pick unripe blueberries

Shut up yer prate = be quiet.

Stay where yer at and I'll come where yer to = stay put until I get there.

"Arn"........ "Narn." = "Did you catch any ? " No, None."

A Noble Fleet Of Sealers   (Anon : Newfoundland, 19[th]Century)

Here's a noble fleet of sealers being fitted for the "ice".
They'll take a chance again this year, tho'the fat's gone down in price.
And the owners will supply them as in the days of old,
for in Newfoundland the SealingVoyage means something more than gold.

The Algerine is first to sail, she's steaming out the harbour.
with eager sealers on her deck, and on the bridge –Wilf Barbour.
The Viking blood runs in his veins , as in the days of yore.
when the Barbours fought the seal and whale , and fished the Labrador.

The Terra Nova's next to sail, in charge of Charlie Kean,
In the history of our fisheries that's a grand and worthy name.
His crew of bully northern men, can handle gaff and gun,
 to get their share , they'll risk and dare, and think it all great fun.

The 'Arctic Sealer's' late to sail, her crew worked with a will, lead by that
modern Jowler, the sealer's friend Sid Hill.
Tho' the last to leave the Harbour , he was first to strike the patches,
and on March the twenty-ninth bore up log loaded to the hatches.

There';s one sailed from Catalina , her owner is Commander,
she's the staunch and sturdy, local built, the good ship 'Newfoundlander'.
When the white coats bawl, he'll risk his all, despite hard luck before,
 for there's ne'er a man in Newfoundland the likes of John Blackmore

And now they're back in old St. John's a-sharing out the flippers,
lets wish good luck to sealers all.
Tho' Newfoundland is changing fast, some things we must not lose,
may we always have our Flipper Pie and Codfish for our Brewis.

Chorus

For the ice is drifting 'suddard' , it's getting near the Funks,
And men will leave their feather beds to sleep in wooden bunks,

 Tho' times are getting hard again our men have not gone soft, They'll haul
their tows o'er icy floes or briskly go aloft.

The Sealer's Song (Anon : Newfoundland 19th Century)

The Block House flag is up today to welcome home the stranger,

And Stewart's house is looking out for Barbour in 'The Ranger',

But Job's are wishing Blanford first who never missed the patches,

He struck them on the 23rd and filled her to the hatches.

And Bowring too will get a few with Jackman in 'The Howler',

The little Kite she bore in sight , with Billy Knee 'The Jowler'.

The first of the fleet is off Torbay, all with their colours flying,

And girls are busy starching shirts and pans of beef steak frying

We left you see with Billy Knee, bound home with colours flying,

We were forced to stay at Trinity Bay two weeks or more there Lyin',

And each Trinity dove fell wild in love with Walsh and Luke McCarthy.

Oh in the spring the flippers bring to lawyers, clerks or beagle,

We fought brave Neptune up and down and carried home 'The Eagle'.

Though some may sing of lords and kings, Brave heros in each Battle,

Our boys for fat, would gaff and bat, and make the whitecoats rattle.

They's kill their foe at every blow (was Waterloo more grander?)

To face who could, an old dog hood, like a plucky Newfoundlander.

We danced on shore in Bremmner's store, the darling girls were dancers,

Jemina Snooks our boys would hook at every set of lancers.

For at a dance no girls can prance , nor dress in style more grander,

For an Irish reel, that takes the heel to please a Newfoundlander.

So here's success to Suzie Bess and girls from all out harbours,

For a kiss set in on a sealer's chin who never saw a barber.

One can see from a reading of the lyrics of these mid to late nineteenth century *Newfoundland* sealing songs, how deeply felt is the sense of pride held by its people in the noble and ubiquitious practice of seal hunting, both inshore and offshore i.e. the famous '*going to the ice*' type. We even see comparisons being made to those of going off to fight in foreign imperial wars of the day and how powerful feelings of valour and national pride are written down and proudly sung about in folk song.

They'll kill their foe at every blow, was Waterloo more grander,

To face who could, an old dog hood, like a plucky Newfoundlander.

It may strike some as odd today that these old-fashioned and outmoded sentiments still seem to persist and thrive in Newfoundland. Yet, this kind of sentiment needs no apology in places like the northern countries of Scandinavia, or Russia, Japan or among other island peoples like those in the Faroe Islands, where a similar strong maritime tradition of hunting whale and seal are found. This seal hunting tradition in *Newfoundland* although originally undertaken solely for domestic purposes, was later expanded into a large and robust industry, to supply the demands of the fashion houses in *London, Paris* and *New York*, when markets for seal fur, especially the whitecoat, opened up there.

Newfoundland has never been a pastoral, farming society, mainly because its coastline isn't a pastoral place and that's where its people settled three and four hundred years ago to pursue the cod fishery, which naturally included a seal fishery when in season. The coastal soil and weather conditions encountered there permitted only the planting and harvesting of crops from small market gardens. As well, a system of indentured servitude grew up between the English merchant class in *St John's* and outport fishermen, during the early period of settlement on the island, in the seventeenth and eighteenth centuries. This was a relationship whereby boats, nets, facilities, (stages, stores) and provisions, were provided to the fishermen in exchange for their catch of cod or other species, and no hard cash changed or rarely changed hands. Thus, when there materilized an opportunity of making some additional (cash) income, however small, through an expanded seal hunt, it was readily grasped by the fishermen.

The harbour in *St. John's* was full of vessels owned by the merchants of the town in those years, and all would be making ready for the annual trip to the ice, with a sailing date generally set for mid to late February. Hundreds of sealers, all desirious of winning a berth on one of these sealing ships, would congregate in *St. John's,* with most having walked for miles, perhaps a hundred or more, from their outport homes. In 1914, the year of the *SS Newfoundland* sealing disaster, 21 vessels sailed from *St. John's* harbour, most being iron clad steamers of 1000 to 2000 tonnes, but the *Newfoundland,* as were many of the others, was a large wooden walled steamer, and for that reason had greater difficulty making progress through the heavy ice pack, than the iron clads. This vulnerability to get stuck in the ice was a contributing factor to the disaster indirectly. To give some idea of the flavour of the times, the 21 ships outward bound from *St. John's* in the 1914 hunt, carried 3700 men, in a town where the population was only around 30,000.

There were two main seal populations to be located and hunted; by far the larger of the two herds was situated on ice floes off the north-east coast of *Newfoundland* and the south coast of *Labrador,* then, and still, refered to as 'the front'. The smaller herd hauled out on ice floes that had squeezed through the *Strait of Belle Isle,* between the mainland *(Labrador)* and the island (Newfoundland), into the *Gulf of St. Lawrence,* known as 'the gulf'. The fleet, after departing St. John's harbour, seperated and set a course for either one or the other of the two locations, with the majority heading for 'the front'. A trip to the ice could last anywhere from a week to 6 or 7 weeks depending on the 'smarts'or luck of the ship's master in locating the seal herds. If lucky and the herd was found quickly, the sealers could *'fill her to the hatches'* with seal pelts in a matter of days. This *'bumper crop',* which all sealers' families prayed for, was then quickly transported back to St.John's and unloaded, then, off they'd go again in high hopes of repeating their good fortune on the second trip. But other captains might not be so lucky, only to find themselves returning to port, after a six or seven week voyage, with a meager catch of hundreds, instead of the thousands of pelts needed to make up a profitable voyage. These indeed could be dark days for the crew. Poor catches likely meant desperate days ahead and instead of set tables only hunger.

The *St. John's* Water St. merchant class dominated *Newfoundland* trade and commerce and controlled it like feudal barrons from the early eighteenth century onwards, although consisting of only a dozen families or so. This dominant economic control of course included every aspect of the fishery including the seal fishery, where in time a huge industry developed, starting very early in the nineteenth and continuing well into the first half of the twentieth century and involving tens of thousands of people. These economic structures and interrelationships were often 'made up' into songs and sung about, with the main characters frequently cropping up in the lyrics of folk songs as in the two printed above. We see there the important family names of the time i.e. the *Bowrings , the Jobs.* etc, and the names of popular or successful vessels and their sealing-ice captains.

A generous affection, or deeply felt reverence is often shown for a vessel i.e. *Terra Nova, Algerine, Arctic Sealer.* Vessels like the *Viking* or *Newfoundland,* are still remembered and honoured a hundred years afterwards, as sealing ships involved in major seal hunt disasters, where tragically large numbers of sealers lost their lives e.g. 78 in the *Newfoundland's* case. After being caught on the ice during a prolonged blizzard, 78 of a party of 135 men from the *Newfoundland,* became lost and perished from exposure. The 57 survivors were only found and rescued three days later. In a more recent disaster which occurred during the 1930s, dozens of sealers were killed by the accidental explosion of a large quantity of dynamite being stored aboard ship, dynamite which was used for breaking through difficult ice jams, as was the case with the *SS Viking.* There is also a brief appearance made in a lyric by the very well known and loved *SS (Northern) Ranger,* a vessel which during the ice free part of the year was more famously employed as a costal steamer, bringing all too infrequent medical and dental care to the many isolated outports of the island and along the Labrador coast, while at the same time supplying these places with life's necessities. Even the large, 2500 tonne ferry *SS Caribou,* which could easily accomadate over 200 and whose ultimate fate was described in some detail earlier in this narrative, pursued the seal hunt on numerous occasions. The names of the sealing captains *Kean, Blanford, Jackman and Barbour,* all commonplace surnames in *Newfoundland,* have found a heroic and permanent place, if sometimes a besmirched one, due to some personal imperfection, in *Newfoundland's* folkore and history. The songs printed here offer lyrics that reflect, often humourously, a simplicity of truth rather than the vague, doubtful metaphor of the poet.

So here's success to Susie Bess and girls from all out-harbours,

For a kiss set in on a sealer's chin, which never saw a barbour.

The seal hunt has become an increasingly controversial and annoyingly provocative business in the post *WW II* years, invariably waxing and waning depending on markets and prices, but also since the 1950s, there's been a growing concern for and an interest in the physical state of the seal herds themselves, with regard to methods of killing, and whether the actual size of the herds are decreasing or maintaining themselves. In an attempt to respond to these concerns, the Federal Government's Committee on Seals and Sealing was struck in the early 1970s, to study the issue surrounding the humane killing of seal pups. It requested Canada's foremost veterinary pathologist and expert on the humane putting down of animals, Dr. Harry Rowsell, to lead this study. In Dr. Rowsell's assessment report, after observing and monitoring the Newfoundland seal hunt over a number of years, he concluded that the method used to kill seal pups by a blow to the head with a club was humane. Moreover, in his opinion, he felt it was more humane than methods used in Toronto at the time, to slaughter lambs. Futhermore, he added that in the Newfoundland seal hunt, there was no waste of animal parts, noting that in addition to taking the pelts, the internal organs and flippers were also harvested for food.

Nevertheless, this widespread interest in and growing concern for animal welfare during the seal hunt, is forcing us all to examine more closely, what it is that we believe, or think and feel, about it. Will the harp seal eventually end up like that of the dodo bird, extinct now for more than a century due to over hunting? Or perhaps, the great northern right whale, which came very close to being hunted to extinction during the nineteenth century? Although this is not likely to happen to the harp seal, in acknowledging our human avarice, hubris and narcissism, we can never be sure, and will have to be constantly vigilant. Sustainable seal hunting has now been going on for hundreds of years in *Newfoundland*, and with continued genuine concern and strict supervision, could continue to do so.

At present, Newfoundlanders are again being made to feel guilt and shame over this aspect of their national life, even being refered to as *'uncivilized'* in some quarters, for such is the absurd language being used by their imperious judges. Are these otherwise hardworking, gentle and affectionate people now to be condemned and forced to wear a *Scarlet Letter* or *Star of David* of their own? I dare not imagine what form it might take. One is left to feel it can only be a *'no–win'* situation for Newfoundlanders and other similar peoples who try to defend a tradition of seal hunting, (whale hunting in Japan and Norway) and explain it effectively to an ever more uncomprending world. It is ironic that the modern, urban populations of *New York, London, Paris* etc. now see things quite differently than did their great-grandparents, who were the original *'fashionistas'* responsible for all this present day commotion in the first place. Our more modern fashionable loungers have a *Disneyesque* attitude, one acquired after years of watching television and viewing movies that deliver a very different message as it relates to animal welfare. Can it be that only rural children or children of the north, be they inuit, aboriginal or white, and be they from whatever nation or background, have an experience that might include the hunting or trapping of wild animals either for their own use and comfort or monetary gain? If only a fraction of the passionate fury and unrelenting rage now spent protesting the seal hunt could be directed towards the very present and real danger threathening the planet by global warming. If lifestyles continue as they are and human populations continue to consume fossil fuels at current rates, the harp seal, the polar bear and other species that depend on a healthy ice floe for mating and reproduction, may be doomed. There might not be a polar ice cap, a glacier covered *Greenland* or sea ice remaining to speak of.

The Miracle Calf

Before taking my leave of this narrative I will relate the tale of the miracle calf. One day while spending a holiday at the outport home of my Aunt Eliza and Uncle Dick, a fellow rushed in to tell them, that a young animal of theirs had fallen off a steep cliff while grazing, unto a rock strewn and sandy bit of shore 70 or 80 feet below. A major problem however was that this area was only accessible by boat. He also told them that the animal appeared to be still alive as far as he could tell, from his vantage point atop the cliff, however, it seemed unable to move. After a family conference which included some neighbouring relatives, it was decided, that they would attempt a rescue. This would necessitate first construcing some kind of sling, in which to transport the steer back to a beach accessible by road, from where their pick-up truck would carry the animal back to their stable. In those days they were still engaged in the fishery, so most of the gear required for the operation was readibly available. *Newfoundland* fishermen and their wives in those days, could still work miracles with the little available to them in the way of materials. Two boats would be needed for the transfer of the animal back from the site of the accident to the *Lower Beach*, which was accessible by road. For the sea going part of the transfer, the sling would be held in place between the two boats by ropes tied to the gunwales. In additiion to the potential danger to the crews by swamping, it would be yet another stressful experience for the young animal to endure, at the time hardly more than a calf, but no other way seemed possible.

I was invited to join four or five of my adult male cousins who would make up the rescue team, even though I was only a boy of twelve. We launched the two rowboats from the *Lower Beach* and set out for the site of the accident which lay above both *Upper and Whelan's Beachs*. With two men rowing each boat, the trip was made quickly in about 30 minutes. We spotted the young steer lying amidst rocks, shrubs, and other litter, quite near the landwash, immediately below a steep cliff whose sloping sides showed signs of recent landslides, but where stunted spruce and other evergreens still managed to cling. Surprisingly, upon closer examination of the young animal, there seemed to be little external trauma caused by the fall, as no deep wounds of any significance were visible. Perhaps this could be explained by the fact that the animal appeared to have had a softer landing than might be expected, cushioned as it was, to a degree, by the large amount of soft earth that had been brought down with it, along with rocks and trees. Very much alive but unable to move, it was nevertheless a pitiful sight.

After some debate and arguing among themselves, my cousins finally agreed upon a modus operandi. The steer was first placed as gentley as possible in the sling, and four of the men transported the animal from where it had fallen, across a short distance of rough terrain to the shore and then out a few feet into the water, where the sling was attached to the gunwales of the two rowboats with several lengths of rope. When it seemed fairly certain that the contraption would hold together and that the patient-passenger it contained would not tumble out during the voyage back to the *Lower Beach,* they set off, rowing with powerful but careful strokes. As the seas were not rough that day, good progress was made and in 45 minutes we were again safely returned to the *Lower Beach,* with a frightened, bewildered and seemingly paralyzed calf.

Finally, there remained the business of transfering the sling and its cargo, to the bed of the pick-up truck, which took up the better part of another hour. Just how the young animal managed to survive all this unfortunate but unavoidable rough handling, including the truck ride over a physically abusive and bone jaring stretch of track, fit for only a horse and cart, remains a mystery. But survive it he did.

By late afternoon we successfully had the calf settled in the barn and made as comfortable as possible. Suspended from an overhead beam which suupported the sling contraption, he was forced to hang for many months in this upright position, for he was quite unable to stand on his own. Sharing the stable with him were three or four other cattle, including the milk cow, whose company he particularily seemed to enjoy and whose attention, to perhaps need. Thus accomadated, all the while receiving plenty of tender loving care, he very slowly but surely began to recover.

His next door neighbour was Barney, the resident farm horse, a friendly, burly, black-coated animal, with a pleasant attitude. No *Newfoundland* pony was this Barney. He had taken me for my *Christmas* holidays from St John's to Aunt Eliza's country home on a number of occassions. I'd hook up with Barney and his handler, my cousin Jim, on late winter afternoons for the 12 mile trip out to their house. With the household provisions stowed aboard, often including a sack of soft, mash grain feed for pigs and cows or a sack of coarse grainy chicken food called 'scratch', upon which we could sit, we'd take off along the usually snow-clogged Thorburn Rd., for the three hour ride. By turns, either stumbling along beside the 'slide' (sled) on the uphill, or riding atop the load on the level and downhill, there'd be no time for stopping because of the severe cold, until we reached Mrs. Alvin Clark's. She was an old widow woman living alone at about the half way point between St. John's and St. Phillips, somewhere near *Windsor Lake*. Here we'd stop for a *'mug-up'* of hot tea and molasses bread, while warming ourselves next to her stove, for perhaps half an hour. Outside, Barney would have a blanket thrown over him and get a small feed of oats to hold him, till we reached home.

I was always especially keen to spend time with my country relatives at this time of year and wanted to get there as quickly as possible, to partake in the *mummering* that would be going on all over the place. The *mummers*, I knew, would be out in full force by six o'clock for an evening of frolicking, pulling pranks and mischief making. I fully intended to get involved in the action both as a *mummer,* (also known thereabouts as *jannies* i.e. *janneying*) or by greeting them from Aunt Eliza's warm kitchen. There were always many small groups of four or five, made up of both young and old, doing the rounds of the houses in the place, black silhouttes outlined against the white snow, and led along from house to house by only the moonlight. From their hiding places among the dark groves of evergreens that lined the roads, older teen-aged boys dressed up like hobby horses or other mythical scary animals, frightened and chased after the girls and children as they came by. We would disguise ourselves when we were out on these rounds, by covering up in sheets, masks and all manner of weird disguises, in our attempts to throw off the guesses of our hosts, as to who we might be. To get a treat or reward, we'd have to perform some song or dance for the crowd gathered in the kitchen, all the while speaking in disguised squeaky voices, or growling like an angry dog. The reward usually was a glass of syrup and a piece of *Christmas* cake for the younger ones, or if grown-up, a glass of blueberry (hert) wine, or shot of rum might be expected, along with the cake. A major difficulty always was how to successfully eat or drink these treats while attempting to maintain the intregity of our camouflages. Such were our outport entertainments during the 12 days of *Christmas,* in the 1940s and the early 1950s.

To return to the poor calf left hanging in his sling from the stable beam. Well, as was said earlier, he was forced to hang in this wretched and uncomfortable contraption for many months before he had recovered enough to stand alone. Almost a year passed before he could venture without assistance outside the barn. By then he could manage a funny, stiff legged kind of walk, or even a little trot. His shape had now also changed somewhat. To go along with his stiff legged gait, he now also possessed a hump, camel like, on his back and what appeared to be a shortened neck. These newly acquired features soon led him to become a *'must see'* attraction in the settlement, eventually bringing back even the vet, to scrutinize, ponder and wonder at our miracle calf, like everybody else.

In the *Newfoundland* of only fifty years ago, one still practiced almost on a daily basis, the old well worn maxim: 'necessity is the mother of invention'. And certainly there would be complete agreement with the words " If you can't sing it, you have to swing it." that the song lyrics to " *Mr. Paganini*' dictate.

To boot, about a year later, our now almost fully grown steer was sold to the slaughterhouse for two or three hundred dollars, which, we are left to hope, made the entire enterprise all worth while.

Codfish

The codfish lays 10,000 eggs, the hen she lays but one,

The codfish she makes ne'er a sound, the hen cackles when she's done,

While the codfish hardly rates a glance, our hen she's such a prize,

Which only goes to show you, that it pays to advertise.

(Anon Newfoundland)

Captioning for Whale Cove Photo Gallery Pictures in Part 4

Page 84:

A)   Map of Nunavut

B): J C giving impromptu concert on tundra at Whale Cove

Page 85:

A) J C's tent on tundra with Whale Cove in background

B) A panaromic view of Whale Cove showing beach, fuel barrels and

inuit shacks

C) A close-up view of inuit one-room shacks in Whale Cove

Page 86:

A): Two Peterhead Whalers hauled out on shore of Whale Cove

B): A Peterhead Whaler left high and dry at low tide on the Whale

Cove beach.

C): Solomon Voisey sitting on beached adult beluga whale

Page 106: Childhood photograph of J C's ninth (?) birthday party taken at St. Thomas', Conception Bay Newfoundland: the boys group . I'm in the middle of the back row.

Page 106 : Childhood photograph of J C's ninth (?) birthday party taken at St. Thomas', Conception Bay, Newfoundland: the boys and girls group. I'm in the top row at right.

Page 107 : Photograph of *MV Theron* making headway in heavy ice off Labrador (March, 1962)

Page 107 : Photograph of 'the cannery' in Whale Cove

Maps: page 2 : Avalon Peninsula; page 23 : Newfoundland and Labrador; page 84 : Nunavut

The Sealer's Song : page 95, A Noble Fleet of Sealers : page 93

Author's note: Instead of using footnotes I have indicated sources within the text.

The song lyrics on pages : 5, 9, 13, 18, 22, 48, 83 and 88 are from

the author's songs.

Some of these may be heard on the CD *'Tea or Tequila'* which is

available on the author's website.

www.johnpchristopher.com   **info@johnpchristopher.com**

ISBN 141209575-1